YORK NOTES

General Editors: Professor A.N. Jeffares (*University of Stirling*) & Professor Suheil Bushrui (*American University of Beirut*)

Evelyn Waugh

DECLINE AND FALL

Notes by Neil McEwan

MA BLITT (OXFORD) PH D (STIRLING)
Lecturer in English,
University of Qatar

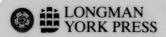

LONGMAN
YORK PRESS

YORK PRESS
Immeuble Esseily, Place Riad Solh, Beirut.

LONGMAN GROUP UK LIMITED
Longman House, Burnt Mill, Harlow,
Essex CM20 2JE, England
Associated companies, branches and representatives
throughout the world

First published 1982
Third impression 1990

ISBN 0-582-02261-4

Produced by Longman Group (FE) Ltd.
Printed in Hong Kong

Contents

Part 1: Introduction   *page* 5
  Life of Evelyn Waugh   5
  General background   7
  Literary background   9
  A note on the text   11

Part 2: Summaries   12
  A general summary   12
  Detailed summaries   14

Part 3: Commentary   35
  Nature, purpose and achievement   35
  Background to composition   39
  Structure   41
  Style   42
  Characterisation   44

Part 4: Hints for study   50
  Study topics   50
  Patterns and themes   52
  Quotations   53
  Arranging material   54
  Specimen questions   55
  Specimen answers   56

Part 5: Suggestions for further reading   64

The author of these notes   66

Part 1

Introduction

Life of Evelyn Waugh

Evelyn Waugh was born in Hampstead, in north London, in 1903. His father, the critic and publisher Arthur Waugh (1866–1943), was a kindly, charming man of letters. After a happy, active childhood, he left home to go as a boarder to Lancing College; like Paul Penny-feather's old school in *Decline and Fall*, Lancing was 'a small public school of ecclesiastical temper on the South Downs'* (in Sussex). Five years later, in 1921, he won a history scholarship to Hertford College, Oxford.

Perhaps because his father and elder brother (the novelist, Alec Waugh, *b*.1898) were writers, Evelyn was attracted in these years to the visual arts: at school he studied calligraphy; at Oxford he made illustrations for student magazines. Charles Ryder, the narrator of Waugh's novel *Brideshead Revisited* (1945), leaves Oxford in mid-course and becomes a successful painter; the undergraduate Waugh would have liked to do the same. He did little academic work but made friends, enjoyed himself and got into debt. After a poor result in his final examinations, he left Oxford in 1924.

He studied art for a while, and hoped to become a craftsman in wood. Instead, he was obliged to teach for a living; he worked, un-happily, in small private schools. Waugh had rich friends, expensive tastes and (before long) an aristocratic fiancée; he began writing—biography and fiction—for money. He published *Rossetti*, a life of the Victorian painter D.G. Rossetti (1828–82), in 1928. Later the same year, Waugh's first novel was an immediate success; this was *Decline and Fall: An Illustrated Novelette* (illustrated, as many of his later books were to be, with his own line drawings). It was followed in 1930 by *Vile Bodies*. These novels established Waugh's reputation as a satirist of fashionable, upper-class English society. After several years of failure—as a student, an artist, a teacher—he had achieved a secure position as a writer.

His private life was more difficult, for a time. His first marriage ended after a year, in 1929. He became a Roman Catholic in 1930, and so was unable to marry again until the Church authorities annulled his broken marriage in 1936. He pressed on with his work. In the course of

Decline and Fall, Penguin Books, Harmondsworth, 1980, p.11.

the 1930s he travelled widely in Africa and South America. He wrote travel books and biography, worked for newspapers, and produced further novels and stories. *Black Mischief* (1932) was based on his visit to Abyssinia (now Ethiopia) in 1930. *A Handful of Dust* (1934) makes use of the author's travels in Brazil. In 1937 Waugh married again. His first son, Auberon, was born in 1939. *Scoop: A Novel about Journalists* (set in Africa) came out in 1938; it was his most entertaining and high-spirited novel since *Decline and Fall*. At the outbreak of the Second World War in 1939, Waugh was prosperously established at his country house in Gloucestershire.

He spent the war as an officer in the Royal Marines and later in the Horse Guards, serving in the Middle East and in Yugoslavia. He entered the army with romantic high hopes of defending civilisation, but ended disillusioned and angered—as a Catholic—by Britain's support for the Yugoslavian communist leader, Tito. After 1945 his conservative views became steadily more rigid. His outlook on life was always satirical. In his early books he ridiculed what he called the 'bogosity' (falseness) of the English 'establishment'. When the literary world came to be dominated in the 1930s and 1940s by left-wing intellectuals, he ridiculed them; and he made enemies.

He had written two novels during the war. *Put out More Flags* (1942) was as pugnaciously satirical as his earlier books. But in *Brideshead Revisited* (1945), he treated upper-class life with humour, sympathy and admiration, and presented religious faith with a serious Catholic purpose. *Brideshead Revisited* was attacked by some critics as a snobbish work, though it was very successful with ordinary readers, especially in America. *The Loved One* (1950), a satire on the luxurious vulgarity of cemeteries in California, increased Waugh's reputation with critics and the public in England and America. But his historical novel *Helena* (1950), a whimsical, witty, devotional work, was said to be lacking in 'contemporary relevance'. Undeterred, Waugh followed his own convictions. The three volumes of his *Sword of Honour* (1952, 1955, 1961), dealing with the fortunes of a Catholic gentleman in the Second World War, were praised for the quality of writing, the lively comedy and the descriptions (based on his own army service) of men at war. They were disparaged too—as *Brideshead Revisited* had been—by readers who found the hero hopelessly out of date.

Waugh had been admired in the 1930s as a young man keenly aware of contemporary life. In the 1950s he seemed behind the times, and even against them; in later life he felt a strong distaste for the modern world. Contempt for modernity is pungently expressed in his short novel *Scott-King's Modern Europe* (1947) and in his fantasy *Love Among the Ruins* (1953). In *The Ordeal of Gilbert Pinfold* (1957), he satirised himself: Pinfold is a pedantic author leading the life of a crusty country squire. Such a role had been attributed to Waugh and he enjoyed acting it out—equipped with a large repertoire of aggressive comic stratagems. These often caused offence, and he was at times cruel to the victims of his highly developed sense of fun.

Towards the end of his life, Waugh was often ill and depressed; but he continued to write well. His *Life* of the Catholic priest and writer Ronald Knox (1888–1957), who had been a close friend, was an elegant biography, published in 1959. Had he lived longer, his work would, by his own account, have been increasingly concerned with religion, though doubtless always entertaining. He died suddenly on Easter Sunday, 1966.

Since his death, the publication of his *Journals* (1973) and *Letters* (1980) has added to his reputation as a major comic writer. Critics still disagree about Waugh. His character—like his books—was complex and unusual; anarchic and irresponsible impulses were merged in him with conservative and strongly held religious beliefs. But there is widespread agreement that his early novels are in the best tradition of English prose satire.

General background

The title of *Decline and Fall* conveys the spirit of the book. It is a joke based on the contrast between the massive work of history by Edward Gibbon (1737–94)—*The Decline and Fall of the Roman Empire* (1776, 1781, 1788)—and the light, fantastic 'novelette' by Evelyn Waugh. Yet behind the joke there is a serious point. Gibbon described history as 'little more than a register of the crimes, follies and misfortunes of mankind'; and he recorded the collapse of Roman civilisation with calm irony. For his part, Evelyn Waugh, in the medium of a short comic novel, depicts with detached amusement the crimes, follies and misfortunes of mankind in the England of his time, and implies that a collapse like that of Rome is not far off. Many writers of the period took the same view. The First World War had put an end to Victorian confidence in the steady progress of society. Lord Circumference asks Paul Pennyfeather, in Part One, Chapter VIII of *Decline and Fall*, if he thinks there is going to be another war. 'Yes, I'm sure of it; aren't you?' Paul replies (p.68). Writing in 1928, Waugh was almost exactly between the two World Wars, and he writes as if he were conscious of it. To the young Evelyn Waugh, English society was amusingly crazy; but he thought its predicament precarious: decline had set in and fall was imminent.

He saw the First World War as the end of an era of relative stability. His father belonged to a generation with secure values, Evelyn thought; the next generation, who had fought in the war, had been crippled. His own post-war contemporaries were living in a 'new world', without guidance from the past. Waugh's second novel, *Vile Bodies*, in which several of the characters from the earlier novel reappear, provides some useful comments on the social world of *Decline and Fall*. The greater freedom of the 'Bright Young People' (as the younger generation of the upper class were known in the newspapers) attracts the envy of the older guests at Margot Metroland's party in Chapter VIII: 'What I always wonder, Kitty dear, is what they actually do at these parties of theirs. I mean do they . . . ?' 'My dear, from all I hear they do'. Waugh wrote about upper-class life because he knew it well; but it gave him the advantage of recording social change where it first started. His characters fly in aeroplanes, drive expensive cars and rebuild their houses in ultra-modern style; they practise a sexual freedom which was not generally accepted in England until the 1960s. (*Decline and Fall* and *Vile Bodies* were thought shocking by many readers when they first appeared). The freedom easily becomes licence and recklessness. Father Rothschild, an intriguing Jesuit, explains the post-war genera-tion to the Prime Minister in *Vile Bodies*: 'these young people say, "If a thing's not worth doing well, it's not worth doing at all." It makes things very difficult for them' (Part Two, Chapter III). That feeling of apathy is behind Margot's frequent use of the word 'boring' in *Decline and Fall*, behind Professor Silenus's peculiarities and Peter Past-master's drunkenness. Boredom, world-weariness and self-indulgence are symptoms, in *Decline and Fall* and *Vile Bodies*, of a malaise behind the gaiety and permissiveness of the 1920s.

Social, artistic and technological change had come very quickly after 1918. Margot's country house, three hundred years old, is torn down and rebuilt (twice) in *Decline and Fall*, a sign of how rapidly the times were changing. Institutions which survived from Victorian England—Oxford, private schools, the Church of England—looked anachronistic in the 1920s to such sharp observers as Evelyn Waugh (although they have, of course, adapted and survived). Life is comically absurd in *Decline and Fall*, often fantastically so; but there was a truly absurd incongruity in England then. Lord Circumference talks of the threat of twentieth century war (in Part One, Chapter VIII) in the terms of a nineteenth-century country gentleman—it upsets life on his estates. Margot Beste-Chetwynde's money—derived at least in part from organised prostitution—makes her a richer woman than the noble Circumferences. Such enormous disparities in wealth as that between Margot and Mrs Grimes had come to seem grotesque. Waugh depicted a mad world in his novel because he sensed that the real world was drastically out of order. Radical adjustments in English life have been made since then. Much that today seems impossibly funny in his early books reflected facts of life in 1928. Nevertheless, if Waugh were alive today he would quickly find out the crimes, follies and misfortunes of the 1980s. Every age, he believed (with Gibbon), is absurd in its own fashion. Journalists sometimes write that 'an Evelyn Waugh is needed' to do justice to some outrageous state of affairs. The comic spirit of *Decline and Fall* is grounded in a type of good sense that we shall always need.

Literary background

Waugh regarded writing as a craft and thought that even the best twentieth-century novelists could hope for nothing more than good craftsmanship: the grand, ambitious projects of nineteenth-century writers were not to be repeated. Clarity, economy and careful design were to be the modern virtues; the craft was to be learned with patience and practised with care. His models can be found in the work of several minor comic prose-writers who achieved these qualities in their own books.

Sir Max Beerbohm (1872-1956) is the most obvious influence. Like Waugh, he illustrated his own work and drew caricatures. A critic and essayist, he also wrote stories, and a novel about Oxford—*Zuleika Dobson* (1911)—in which satire and wit are mixed with fantasy. Waugh admired and imitated the precision with which Beerbohm planned his stories; he also seems to have copied his use of an apparent naïvety in the narrator as a satirical weapon.

Beerbohm was a friend of Oscar Wilde (1854-1900); both were dandies in their lives and in their writing. Waugh admired dandified elegance, natural or artificial; and the style of *Decline and Fall* some-times recalls the epigrams and paradoxes of Wilde's plays. Dr Fagan's advice when Paul arrives at his school might have come from one of Wilde's characters: 'We schoolmasters must temper discretion with deceit' (Part One, Chapter II). Waugh's skills with plotting and dia-logue were perhaps improved by his knowledge of Wilde. Waugh's use of dialogue as a means of developing the story was certainly influ-enced by the witty, exotic tales of Ronald Firbank (1886-1926). Firbank's work also taught him the art of omitting all but the essential in presenting a scene or a part of the story. Waugh shares his delight in extravagance, in setting and in plot, with Beerbohm, Wilde and Fir-bank. They are sometimes classed as 'Aesthetes'—writers who prefer beauty in literature to serious purpose. Waugh was in many respects a serious man, but he adopted their practice of rejecting solemn critical claims in speaking of his own books. Harold Acton (*b*.1904), the friend to whom *Decline and Fall* is dedicated, was a prominent aesthete at Oxford, and he too influenced this element in Waugh's make-up.

Hector Hugh Munro (1870-1916), who wrote short stories and a novel under the pseudonym 'Saki', is another model. Munro's best writing has the caustic pungency we find in *Decline and Fall*. Waugh's ingenious comic imagination, his wit, his relish for ruthlessness in his characters, and his inclination towards violent and cruel events,—his 'black' comedy—are all reminiscent of Saki. A student of *Decline and Fall* might read the opening chapters of Saki's novel *The Unbearable Bassington* (1912) to judge Waugh's debt for himself.

The influence of the Catholic writer Hilaire Belloc (1870-1953) is of a different kind. His poems, essays and stories are lively and often very funny. But there is a serious mind behind his work, and a view of present events in the perspective of eternity. Waugh came to believe, as Belloc did, that the follies and misfortunes of any generation are to be expected from the nature of Man, and that consolation can be found only in religious belief. Waugh admired Belloc, and when he met him, in 1932, he was on his best behaviour; afterwards, when asked what he thought of the younger author, Belloc replied: 'He is *possessed*'.* There is a demonic element in *Decline and Fall*, as in most of Waugh. He was obliged, as a Catholic, to fight it in his life, but he profited as a writer. Waugh had a religious sense of evil which he conveyed in comedy. Belloc among others taught him how to do so.

Although, like most of his contemporaries, Waugh set out to be anti-Victorian, the Victorians were a part of his literary background. He grew up hearing the novels of Charles Dickens (1812-70) read aloud by his father (who read them very well). The grotesque but vital figure of Pennyfeather's colleague Captain Grimes owes something to Dickens. W.M. Thackeray (1811-63), the satirist and ironist who wrote *Vanity Fair* (1848), may have helped to form Waugh's view of social vanities. The fantasy of Thackeray's early stories no doubt pleased the young Waugh. *Decline and Fall* echoes Dickens and Thackeray in its use of whimsical names, for example. In his sense of comic possibilities and power to develop them, Waugh can be seen as one of their successors.

He was equally familiar with Victorian poetry. Alastair Digby-Vane-Trumpington stands, watching Paul's boat draw away from the coast, 'like Sir Bedivere' (Part Three, Chapter VI). Although this is a mocking allusion to *The Idylls of the King* (1889) by Alfred Lord Tennyson (1809-92), the romanticism of Tennyson's poetry was attractive to Waugh. He ridicules the mannered, precious prose style of Walter Pater (1839-94) at the end of Part Three, Chapter V, in Paul's reflections on the death of Grimes, but he liked such writing and enjoyed mimicking it. In this he resembles the poet T.S. Eliot (1888-1965). They both wished to break away from Romantic literature and create a modern mode of writing more suited to the harsh twentieth century.

*Christopher Sykes, *Evelyn Waugh: A Biography*, Collins, 1975, p.126.

But the works of both Waugh and Eliot were affected by Romanticism, none the less.

In some ways *Decline and Fall* is obviously unlike such works of the 'Modernist' movement as Eliot's poem *The Waste Land* (1922) and the novel *Ulysses* (1922) by James Joyce (1882-1941). They are more experimental in technique and more sombre in outlook. *Decline and Fall* can be seen as a traditional type of story. Paul Pennyfeather's adventures might recall those of the naïve hero in *Candide* (1759) by the French satirist Voltaire (François Marie Arouet, 1694-1778). But Waugh's novel belongs to the period of *Ulysses* and *The Waste Land*. It conveys, as they do, the instability of the post-Victorian world. It too is based on wide reading but reveals a new, unmistakable talent.

A note on the text

Decline and Fall: An Illustrated Novelette was first published in London by Chapman and Hall in 1928, with Waugh's line drawings. This edition has been frequently reprinted. A paperback edition was first issued by Penguin Books, Harmondsworth in 1937; it has been constantly reprinted.

Part 2

Summaries
of DECLINE AND FALL

A general summary

Paul Pennyfeather is a serious-minded young man, studying at Oxford to become a clergyman. One evening, returning to his college rooms, he is attacked by a group of drunken aristocrats who are holding a Club dinner. They mistake the colours of his tie for those of their Club and strip him of tie and trousers. Next day they are fined by the college authorities; he is expelled for indecent behaviour: running through college *'without trousers!'*

Paul (who is still under twenty-one) goes home to consult his legal guardian. He is told he must now work for a living. He calls at a scholastic agency where a Dr Fagan, of Llanabba Castle School in Wales, recruits him as a teacher.

Llanabba School is situated in a large country house. The castle's architecture is sham, and so is Dr Fagan. Although the headmaster is obsessed by the question of social status in his pupils and staff, his two daughters (called 'Flossie' and 'Dingy' by the boys) are startlingly vulgar. He has two other masters: a former clergyman called Prendergast who is too feeble to keep order; and the grotesque Captain Grimes who has passed through many schools, always in trouble. Paul gets to know an influential boy called Peter Beste-Chetwynde, whom he is supposed to teach to play the organ (though unable to play it himself). Prendergast tells him about his religious doubts; Grimes talks shamelessly about his sexual perversions; at Llanabba he currently has a 'favourite', a boy called Clutterbuck. The school butler, Philbrick, gives various glamorous, implausible accounts of his real identity.

Lady Circumference comes to visit her son Tangent; Dr Fagan organises a Sports Day at short notice. Mrs Beste-Chetwynde, rich but notorious, is among the guests; Paul finds her attractive. The sports are a failure. Mrs Beste-Chetwynde brings her latest young man, a negro who provokes racialist comments from the parents. Mr Prendergast, drunk, accidentally shoots young Lord Tangent with a starting-pistol. (The boy's foot has to be amputated and he later dies.) Afterwards Mrs Beste-Chetwynde writes to Peter suggesting that Paul tutor him in the holidays. Meanwhile Grimes has been caught misbehaving with Clutterbuck; he marries Dr Fagan's elder daughter to preserve his job. Philbrick has been fraudulently enjoying credit in the district by posing as 'Sir Solomon Philbrick'; when the police arrive he has disappeared. Grimes, who cannot bear life in Dr Fagan's family circle, disappears soon afterwards, leaving a suicide note. The school holidays begin.

Paul goes with Peter to King's Thursday, the Beste-Chetwynde's country house. The former Tudor building has recently been demolished and an ultra-modern construction designed by the German architect Otto Silenus. The new house is spectacular but scarcely suited to human habitation (it is to be torn down before long). Margot Beste-Chetwynde's wealth is boundless; her friends and way of life are upper-class and eccentric.

Paul and Margot become engaged. Part of Margot's money comes from her 'business' which involves sending prostitutes to South America. An Oxford friend of Paul's called Arthur Potts is investigating her activities on behalf of the League of Nations. Paul, naïvely unaware of what Margot is doing, is sent to Marseilles to assist in the transit of a group of girls bound for Argentina (where Grimes, meanwhile, has found a job). On his return, and just before the wedding, he is arrested.

Peter visits him as he awaits trial. One of Margot's previous suitors, Sir Humphrey Maltravers, the Home Secretary, is prepared to arrange Paul's escape if Margot will marry him. She is willing but Paul is not. His sentence is seven years, for traffic in prostitutes. In gaol he meets Philbrick, and also Prendergast, who is now the prison chaplain. The Governor, a man of progressive but misguided ideas, irritates Paul; but otherwise he enjoys prison. Its calm is interrupted when a deranged prisoner, whom the Governor has provided with carpentry tools, decapitates Prendergast with a saw.

Paul is transferred to a second prison where he meets Grimes, who has been convicted of bigamy (his first wife turned up in Argentina). Grimes escapes and is, once again, presumed dead. Margot visits Paul, telling him that she means to marry Maltravers. His conditions begin to improve; books, good food and wine are provided. Before long he is sent away for an operation, on the Home Secretary's instructions. The seaside clinic is run by Dr Fagan. Margot's latest young man, Alastair Trumpington—one of the Oxford rioters who caused Paul's expulsion—has arranged for a disreputable doctor to sign a false death certificate. Once 'dead', Paul leaves on Margot's yacht. Maltravers (now Lord Metroland) has kept his word.

After a period at Margot's villa on a Greek island where he finds Silenus, Paul returns, disguised by a moustache, to Oxford and resumes his previous studies. Meeting Peter (now Lord Pastmaster), he agrees that he should never have become mixed up with such people as the Beste-Chetwyndes. They are 'dynamic', he says (using a distinction Silenus has taught him); he is 'static'. He means in future to lead a safe and orthodox life.

Detailed summaries

Prelude

The Bollinger Club has been holding a dinner-party at Scone College, Oxford. This is a rare event because the wild, drunken behaviour of its aristocratic members usually results in the club's suspension for several years afterwards. Most of the academic staff have moved out of college for safety. The two who remain are looking on from a distance as the club members vandalise the rooms of unpopular students. The dons watch eagerly, hoping for damage to property: if the fines levied next day rise above fifty pounds, the best port-wine in the cellars will be served in celebration. 'O, please God,' says the Junior Dean, 'make them attack the Chapel'.

Paul Pennyfeather, an earnest, sober undergraduate, returning to his rooms in college, is wearing the tie of his old school, whose colours unluckily resemble those of the Bollinger Club. The rioters mistake it for their own, take offence, and strip Paul of most of his clothes. Next morning the Bollinger members are fined; but Paul, who was seen running through college without his trousers, is expelled for indecent behaviour.

NOTES AND GLOSSARY:

Junior Dean: college official responsible for student discipline

Domestic Bursar: college treasurer

Scone College: Oxford University is made up of colleges in which students live and work. Scone College is an invention; it was at Scone in Scotland that Scottish kings were crowned

senior members . . . dons: academic staff

Bollinger Club: in reality, the Bullingdon Club. Bollinger is the name of a champagne

Boar's Hill and North Oxford: residential districts of Oxford

lairds: country gentry in Scotland

London season: the months when the aristocracy took up residence in London

débutantes: girls who have just 'come out', that is, have been formally presented to the queen and are enjoying their first London 'season'

Matisse: Henri Matisse (1869–1954), distinguished French painter

Ramsay MacDonald: (1866–1937) Prime Minister in the first Labour government, 1924

Dean . . . Master: the most senior college officials

House: public schools are organised in boarding 'houses'
preparatory school: small private school for younger boys where they are prepared for their public schools
Hall: college dining hall
League of Nations: the principal International organisation, 1919-46
Forsyte Saga: a series of novels by John Galsworthy (1866-1933)
Thomas More Society: More (1478-1535) was the author of *Utopia* (1516)
scholar: a student who has won a college award by examination and is expected to behave seriously
battels: college bill
Stanley's *Eastern Church:* Dean A.P. Stanley (1815-81) wrote *Lectures On The Eastern Church* (1861)
Dr Johnson: Samuel Johnson (1709-84), poet, critic and moralist
becoming a schoolmaster: before Oxford Paul was at a *public* school: a fee-paying boarding-school for teenage boys. He could not expect—without a degree—to find a post in a school of this kind. They were larger and (though austere and often eccentric) more respectable than the *private* school for which Paul is recruited in the next chapter. For more on the English school system, see the section on 'Background to composition' in Part 3, Commentary, below

---

Part One, Chapter I Vocation

Paul returns to his guardian's home in London. He has been studying to be a clergyman, but his disgrace has made a career in the Church impossible. His guardian is unsympathetic; indeed, he exploits Paul's predicament by stopping his allowance and spending the money on his own daughter. Paul will have to work for his living, and the only prospect, it appears, for a young man sent down from university for indecent behaviour is a teaching job in a private school.

'Church and Gargoyle' is a scholastic agency which supplies such schools with teachers. It has on its books a post at Llanabba Castle School in Wales, where the headmaster, Dr Augustus Fagan, requires an experienced, well-qualified master. Paul is unqualified and without experience, but the agency explains that Dr Fagan cannot expect much for the money offered. The headmaster, undismayed by Paul's youth and recent expulsion, offers him the job at a reduced salary. Fagan speaks grandly of his school's ideals, but appears to be chiefly concerned with 'tone'; that is, with the social status of his pupils and staff. Paul is to start the following evening.

NOTES AND GLOSSARY:
Gilbert and Sullivan: comic operas by Sir W.S. Gilbert (1836–1911) and Sir Arthur Sullivan (1842–1900)
ninety pounds a year: Waugh's first teaching post paid £150 a year
tone: social distinction
not out of the top drawer: vulgar, common
five per cent: the agency takes a percentage of Paul's salary

Part One, Chapter II Llanabba Castle

The school is housed in a country mansion which has been partially rebuilt, with sham castle battlements, in the nineteenth century. Paul arrives at night and is shown to the masters' Common Room by a supercilious butler. Here he sits waiting among books, gowns and sticks. Boys come in from time to time and stare at him, giggling. A master appears briefly—a short, balding young man with a red moustache and an artificial leg. This is Captain Grimes. Grimes rebukes a boy for whistling and tells Paul that the school lacks discipline. Later an older master, Prendergast, tells Paul that he is sure to hate the school. Prendergast has hated it for ten years.

Summoned to see Dr Fagan, Paul meets the headmaster's daughters: the elder is gaily dressed and vulgar; the younger grim and concerned about economies. Dr Fagan outlines Paul's teaching. He is, among other duties for which he is unqualified, to give organ lessons to a boy called Beste-Chetwynde. Fagan advises him to say nothing about why he left Oxford.

NOTES AND GLOSSARY:

Bangor:	a coastal town in North Wales
cotton famine:	the American Civil War (1861–5) affected the cotton industry of Lancashire; the cotton-workers were obliged to rebuild Llanabba, cheaply, for its Victorian owner. Waugh is attacking (in this paragraph) Liberal principles of 'enlightened self-interest' on the part of Victorian property-owners
rococo:	overelaborate in pattern
Tartar:	here, a ruthlessly stern person

Part One, Chapter III Captain Grimes

In the dining-room Paul meets Beste-Chetwynde. Recalling Dr Fagan's advice that schoolmasters must 'temper discretion with deceit', Paul claims to be an expert organist. Beste-Chetwynde seems very self-confident; he and Paul begin to be friends. After dinner Paul goes out with Captain Grimes to drink at Mrs Robert's public house. Grimes talks with a cheery frankness about himself and the school. He lost his leg in a road accident, when drunk (not in the war as the boys suppose). The Fagan daughters, Florence and Diana, are known as Flossie and Dingy. Grimes is secretly engaged to Flossie, the elder, and means to announce it when next in trouble. He is often in trouble ('in the soup') and has survived a lifetime of scandals in war and peace, largely thanks to his status as 'a public-school man'. Temperament and sex have been his weaknesses, he says. But when the school butler, Philbrick, who is present in the bar, offers to introduce either of them to a girl, Grimes's comment implies that he is not interested in women.

NOTES AND GLOSSARY:

Eton suits: suits with short jackets and wide collars
rotting: (*schoolboy slang*) joking, kidding
combinations: long underwear
per Christum . . .: 'for Jesus Christ Our Lord', part of a Latin prayer ('grace') said at meal times
Stoke-on-Trent: a northern industrial town
one-over-the-eight: drunk
public-school man: the large, expensive boarding schools known as public schools in England conferred a sharper social distinction fifty years ago than today. Podger's is the name of Grimes's former house at Harrow, a major school of this type
Harrovian: a pupil of Harrow

Part One, Chapter IV Mr Prendergast

Beste-Chetwynde wakes Paul and advises him to secure the masters' bathroom before Mr Prendergast can reach it; Paul does so. After breakfast, Prendergast is sadly resigned to his defeat; he seems defeated by life. He tells Paul how he used to be a clergyman, living comfortably in a vicarage and looked after by his mother, when he began to suffer religious doubts. He could not understand why God made the world at all. Nowadays, having left the Church, his only consolation is his collection of pipes.

NOTES AND GLOSSARY:

Charvat: an expensive Paris firm
a living: a clergyman's post
Reservation: the practice of preserving the bread of the eucharist
Lady Chapel: a small chapel dedicated to the Virgin Mary, built as an extension to a large church

Cain's wife: see the Bible, Genesis 4:17; the problem is of her identity, because Cain was the son of Adam, the first man

Archbishop Parker: Matthew Parker (1504–75) was the first Anglican (Protestant) Archbishop of Canterbury consecrated under Queen Elizabeth I in 1559

Tower of Babel: see the Bible, Genesis 11:1–10

Babylonian captivity: see the Bible, 2 Kings 25

Part One, Chapter V Discipline

Morning prayers are said in the panelled hall. Grimes assures Paul that he never suffers doubts but is 'in harmony with the primitive promptings of humanity'. Dr Fagan, in his doctoral robes, makes several announcements. A boy has been caught smoking cheap cigars in the boiler-room—not a gentlemanly fault. Grimes whispers to Paul that he gave the cigars to Clutterbuck; this 'nasty little boy' (according to Prendergast) appears to be Grimes's favourite.

In his classroom Paul has trouble keeping order until Grimes looks in and lends him a stick. Paul adopts a firmer tone. The boys are to write an essay on self-indulgence. There will be a small prize for the longest, irrespective of merit (Clutterbuck wins). Prendergast is envious of Paul's success. He never manages to keep order: the boys make fun of his wig.

During a music lesson, Paul learns from Beste-Chetwynde that he is now popular with his form. The boys think there is something mysterious about Philbrick: he wears diamond rings. Perhaps he is a Russian prince? Paul thinks not.

NOTES AND GLOSSARY:

baronial: in mock-medieval style

half a crown: twelve and a half pence in the new currency

vox humana: (*Latin*) human voice; a stop on the organ

Pop goes the weasel: an irreverent song

Russians: titled Russians who had fled from the Revolution

Part One, Chapter VI Conduct

Paul arrives at an understanding with his form: they keep quiet during class in return for an undemanding course of work. Rain makes organised games impossible, and Paul enjoys life more than he expected. In the evenings Grimes entertains him with stories of his outrageous sexual adventures. Prendergast is wretched as usual.

A letter comes from Oxford. One of Paul's friends, Arthur Potts, tells him that Sir Alastair Digby-Vane-Trumpington, a Bollinger Club member, has offered him twenty pounds in compensation for his mistreatment on the night of the dinner. Paul decides that his duty is to refuse; he considers himself a gentleman of the middle class, not an irresponsible aristocrat as Trumpington is. But Grimes, anticipating Paul's integrity, has telegraphed Potts to send the money. It comes several days later. Paul and Grimes agree to invite Prendergast to join them in a celebration dinner at the nearest town.

NOTES AND GLOSSARY:

J.C.R.:	Junior (Student) Common Room
set:	group of friends
rubbings:	wax impressions taken from brasses in a church
O.S.C.U.:	Oxford Student Christian Union
new methods:	the progressive speculations about education in Potts's letters are far removed from the everyday life of Llanabba
binge:	informal dinner-party, with drinks
Cwmpryddyg:	intended as a typical Welsh place-name

Part One, Chapter VII Philbrick

The rain eases. Dr Fagan announces that the Annual Sports will take place tomorrow. Paul is to be in charge of arrangements. The headmaster has ambitious plans; music, champagne and fireworks are to be laid on. Lady Circumference, mother of the school's most aristocratic pupil Lord Tangent, will distribute the prizes. Mrs Beste-Chetwynde is coming too: she is the richest parent, though not free from scandal; according to rumour, she poisoned her husband. It becomes clear that these important visitors are the sole reason for the sports.

During the preparations, Philbrick tells Paul about his past life: an unlikely story of a successful criminal career. He came to Llanabba, he admits, intending to kidnap Lord Tangent. Since then he has fallen in love with the younger Miss Fagan, whose skill in saving money will be useful at the public house he owns in London.

Prendergast fails to run off the heats: the boys feel cold and simply disappear, probably to change. Grimes invents the 'results' by the common-room fire. Clutterbuck appears to have done very well.

NOTES AND GLOSSARY:

the General Strike: this took place in England in 1926
Eisteddfod: Welsh festival of arts
across the river: south of the Thames, in London

Lambeth:	a district of south London
V.C.:	Victoria Cross, the highest military award for valour
the Dardanelles:	a campaign on the Dardanelles straights in 1915
Llandudno:	a Welsh seaside town

Part One, Chapter VIII The Sports

Next day the rain still holds off. Dr Fagan and his staff appear in an assortment of outfits; Prendergast wears a sporting blazer. Fagan admits to Paul that such occasions have always been disastrous failures in the past.

The grotesque appearance of the musicians in the silver band provokes an impassioned monologue from Dr Fagan on the alleged weaknesses of the Welsh character. Paul is introduced to Lord and Lady Circumference. They are tough-minded, old-fashioned country landowners. Lady Circumference tells Paul that her son needs constant beating. Her husband grumbles about the sad effects of the last war on his estates. He and Paul agree that another war will come soon—this time, Paul thinks, against the Americans. The Circumferences learn that Paul has 'met' their nephew Alastair Trumpington.

The races begin badly. Prendergast, who has been to Mrs Roberts's pub with Grimes and is now drunk, shoots little Lord Tangent in the foot with a loaded starting-pistol provided by Philbrick. In the background the silver band plays sacred music. A quarrel breaks out between Lady Circumference and the lower-middle-class Clutterbuck family when Clutterbuck is accused of cheating by running one lap too few in the three-mile race.

Driving up in a vast limousine, the beautiful Mrs Beste-Chetwynde arrives with her latest young man, Chokey. Although graceful and perfectly dressed, Chokey creates a stir among the provincial guests who are surprised at meeting a Negro.

NOTES AND GLOSSARY:

jeune premier:	(*French*) young leading-man in a play
Ascot:	horse races at Ascot in Berkshire, attended by the fashionably dressed
keep wicket:	at cricket
in khaki:	in the army, in uniform
Hispano Suiza:	an expensive make of car
We are the silver band . . .:	the stationmaster speaks in an exaggerated version of Welsh English
Edward of Caernarvon:	King Edward II (1307–27), a corrupt, ineffectual ruler

the Tudors: the Tudor monarchs who ruled England in the late fifteenth and sixteenth centuries came from Wales

dissolution of the Church: the breaking-up of the medieval Catholic organisation of the Church in the sixteenth century

Lloyd George: David Lloyd George (1863–1945) was Liberal Party Leader and Prime Minister

chaffing: teasing

doin'... beatin'... shockin': upper-class pronunciation

hunters: horses bred and kept for hunting

the farms: Lord Circumference owns a number of them

the Crick at Rugby: cross-country running at Rugby school

licked: beaten

Potts!:   this name, unlike those she has mentioned, sounds common to her

Men of Harlech: an old, patriotic Welsh song

tight: drunk

bounder: not a gentleman

Apostolic Claims: the claim of the Ethiopian Church to have been founded by Christ's apostles

Champs-Elysées: a broad avenue in Paris

Part One, Chapter IX The Sports—continued

Paul serves sandwiches in the refreshment tent. The guests are divided over the result of the three-mile race: a Clutterbuck party is opposed to a Circumference party. Chokey's presence arouses racialist observations from Philbrick and Mrs Clutterbuck and from a Colonel Sidebotham who is apprehensive, recalling his days of colonial warfare. Lady Circumference is made uneasy by the richer, more cosmopolitan Mrs Beste-Chetwynde. Waugh satirises the racialist prejudices of the guests, the tourist's enthusiasm of Chokey (who likes cathedrals), and Mrs Beste-Chetwynde whose relationship with Chokey is inspired by a fashionable love of the exotic. Meanwhile the band has been playing the same song for over half an hour. It is the only non-religious piece they know, and to play sacred music, they claim, would be blasphemous so long as Mrs Beste-Chetwynde is smoking cigarettes. A pound note, added to their fee, changes their minds.

The variety of cultures—Welsh, aristocratic English, London East End (in Philbrick), and black American—with its resulting mixture of prejudices—is used to make this a maliciously funny chapter.

NOTES AND GLOSSARY:

the Boxer rising: the Chinese 'Boxer' secret society attacked the foreign legations in Pekin in 1900

too expensive:	Mrs Beste-Chetwynde has a grander idea of expense than Lady Circumference, and they both know it
Cholmondley:	a distinctly English family name (pronounced Chumly)
Salisbury:	a southern English cathedral town
Sion:	Zion; the meaning is 'religious songs'
In Thy courts . . .:	religious music; see the Bible, Revelation 21:23

Part One, Chapter X Post Mortem

Dr Fagan has been disappointed by Sports Day. Mr Prendergast has quarrelled with Chokey over a question of church architecture. Lady Circumference has been rude about the three-mile race in her speech at the prize-giving.

In the common-room Prendergast is still drunk. He is sent off to take evening preparation while Grimes and Paul leave for Mrs Roberts's. Paul is interested in Mrs Beste-Chetwynde, and jealous of Chokey. Grimes decides that Paul is in love.

Back at school Prendergast looks pleased with himself. He has just caned twenty-three boys.

NOTES AND GLOSSARY:

rood-screen:	a screen, surmounted by a cross (or rood) between the choir and the nave of a church
Thomas Hardy:	English novelist and poet (1840–1928)
Reigate:	a small country town in Surrey, in the south of England
Ding, dong, dell . . .:	from a children's song
frisson . . . Je ne sais quoi:	(*French*) thrill of pleasure . . . that uncertain feeling
Prep.:	preparation; set work for evening study in a boarding school

Part One, Chapter XI Philbrick—continued

Next day the three masters discuss Philbrick, who has given each of them a different, highly romantic account of himself. To Prendergast he has represented himself as a shipowner; to Grimes as a novelist; to Paul as a burglar. All three stories are improbable.

NOTES AND GLOSSARY:

Athenaeum Club:	a distinguished London club, founded in 1824; its members are usually connected with the arts or sciences

the first crusade: European war against the Islamic Middle East in
the eleventh century
Chelsea: a district of south-west London favoured by artists
and poets

Part One, Chapter XII The Agony of Captain Grimes

Tangent's foot has swollen and turned black, Beste-Chetwynde glee-
fully reports to Paul at the next music lesson. Beste-Chetwynde reads a
letter from his mother suggesting that Paul ('the good-looking young
master') come as his tutor for the holidays.

Paul goes to share this good news with Grimes, but finds him depressed, for once. He is 'in the soup' again—presumably having been
caught misbehaving with Clutterbuck—and has had to save his job
by announcing his engagement to Flossie. There is a complication,
however. Grimes is, he confesses to Paul, married already.

Dr Fagan sends for Paul that evening and outlines the situation. With
all the dignity and tact that he can muster, he suggests that Paul marry
Flossie. He offers a partnership with a thousand pounds a year, but is
not surprised when Paul refuses. 'It must be Grimes, then,' he concludes.

Paul asks Grimes what he would like as a wedding present. Grimes
reminds him of the proposal to dine out in Cwmpryddyg on Trumpington's money. The next evening Paul and Prendergast take him to the
Hotel Metropole, where they find Philbrick, who promises ('one day')
to tell his true story which is 'stranger than any fiction'. Philbrick leaves,
but champagne is offered by the waiter—with the compliments of Sir
Solomon Philbrick.

Grimes is depressed for a while by the prospect of domestic life,
though he cheers up later. Prendergast cannot understand why anyone
ever marries.

NOTES AND GLOSSARY:
huitres: (*French*) oysters
Jeroboam: a very large bottle
other two advantages: begetting children; and 'mutual society, help and
comfort'

Part One, Chapter XIII The Passing of a Public School Man

Grimes and Flossie are married. Everyone from the school is present
except Dr Fagan, for whom 'the whole business is too painful', and
Lord Tangent, whose foot is being amputated in hospital. Dr Fagan
gives twenty-five pounds as a wedding present. The boys give a teapot.
Grimes's first (Irish) wife does not intervene. That evening Grimes and

Paul go to Mrs Roberts's as usual and Grimes buys drinks for everyone. Then Grimes returns to his new life in the Doctor's part of the Castle.

When he visits the masters' common-room a few days later, he complains that Dr Fagan humiliates him, making him feel inferior. He feels demoralised, a failure. Next day a letter comes from Mr Clutterbuck, who is a brewer, offering him a job as a beer-taster. Grimes is tempted to accept and leave the Fagans.

Police inspectors call at the school looking for Philbrick, who is wanted on charges of false pretences and impersonation; he has been passing himself off as a rich man at big hotels. Philbrick has disappeared. Three days later Grimes disappears too, leaving a note with his clothes by the seashore: 'Those that live by the flesh shall perish by the flesh'. It is assumed that he has drowned himself. The school breaks up for the holidays.

NOTES AND GLOSSARY:

a slight injury: a convenient fiction, of course, since Paul cannot play the organ

art nouveau: curvilinear style of decoration fashionable at the beginning of the century

forbid the banns: object to the marriage (on grounds of bigamy)

D.T.'s: *delirium tremens*, a condition induced by alcohol poisoning

live by the flesh: see the Bible, Romans 8:13

Part Two, Chapter I King's Thursday

The head of the Beste-Chetwynde family is Lord Pastmaster. Their Tudor house, King's Thursday, has remained unaltered for centuries until recently, when Lord Pastmaster was obliged to sell it to Mrs Beste-Chetwynde. She has had it torn down and rebuilt, in ultra-modern style and materials, by a daring young 'futurist' architect she has discovered, 'Professor' Otto Silenus. Silenus holds that domestic architecture cannot be beautiful because the human element contaminates: he aims to eliminate that, as far as possible.

NOTES AND GLOSSARY:

William and Mary: King William III and Queen Mary II ruled England from 1689. Mary died in 1694; William in 1702

Bond Street and Park Lane: in the centre of fashionable London

Bloody Mary: Queen Mary I, 1553-8, so called because of her treatment of Protestants

Prayer Book: the Book of Common Prayer was composed in the sixteenth century

Hanse: a group of trading cities in Germany from the Middle Ages until the nineteenth century

the traditional character of his family: not sentimental or nostalgic, but practical and adventurous

Mr Jack Spire in the *London Hercules:* Waugh does not seem to sympathise here with the imaginary journalist's attempt to preserve the house

Cincinnati: in Ohio, in the American Middle-West

Teneat Bene . . .: (*Latin*) May the family hold on to it!

Silenus: the name, in Greek mythology, belongs to a jovial old satyr

Bloomsbury: a district of London favoured by intellectuals

Part Two, Chapter II Interlude in Belgravia

Paul dines in London with Arthur Potts. The narrator intervenes in the story to tell us that the real Paul Pennyfeather, a normal, competent young man, comes to life for this one evening of comfortable security: the character we see in the novel is only his shadow.

Potts discusses Otto Silenus's work. Paul tells him about Llanabba. Potts has left Oxford to take up 'rather an interesting job' with the League of Nations. Next day the 'real' Paul 'disappears' again into his 'shadow-life' as hero of the novel.

NOTES AND GLOSSARY:

Belgravia: a smart district of south-west London

Byzantine mosaics: the art of Byzantium (centre of the eastern Roman empire) was in fashion in the 1920s

Bauhaus at Dessau: the Bauhaus, a German centre for modern artists and technicians, moved from Weimar to Dessau in 1925; it was widely influential in architecture.

Corbusier: Le Corbusier (Charles-Edouard Jaenneret, 1887–1965), Swiss architect, a pioneer of modern styles and materials

Manchester School: utilitarians of the nineteenth century, associated with free trade; regarded as vulgar by such young men of the 1920s as Paul and Potts

Schools: final degree examinations at the University of Oxford

---

Part Two, Chapter III Pervigilium Veneris

Paul travels with Peter Beste-Chetwynde from London to King's Thursday. Among the chestnut trees in the grounds of the house, Paul has a vision of the permanence and tradition of English rural life. This is suddenly dispelled when the house, rebuilt by Silenus, comes into view.

Mrs Margot Beste-Chetwynde is sitting at a table of vulcanite, on a floor of green glass. 'Professor' Otto Silenus is there. They discuss the new house. The architect declares that he hates his own work. Peter Beste-Chetwynde likes it. His mother withdraws, in the aluminium lift.

Paul tells Silenus that he thinks Margot the most wonderful woman in the world. Silenus thinks her much like any other woman, and aesthetically displeasing in so far as she differs from the average. Otherwise, he would have married her (she asked him to, twice). In ten years, he says, speaking of her as though she were a machine, she will be 'almost worn out'.

Next morning Paul looks out from the vita-glass windows on to the half-finished terrace of silver and scarlet. Margot keeps to her room. Peter receives the week-end guests. The visitors are from the most unconventional circles of upper-class London—'Mayfair'. (Miles Malpractice and David Lennox the photographer are homosexuals, and so, presumably, are Pamela Popham and Olivia.) Guests continue to arrive at all hours of day and night.

Sir Humphry Maltravers, the 'Minister of Transportation', is the only newcomer to comment on Margot's prolonged absence. He discusses Margot with Paul. He disapproves of the new house. Margot should marry someone (like himself) with a position in public life. Like Prendergast, Grimes and Philbrick, he is eager to tell Paul the story of his life. From humble origins he has risen to his present eminence by hard work.

After the guests' departure, Margot reappears, 'fresh and exquisite'. She needs to marry, she says: Maltravers wishes to marry her. Before long, Paul asks her to marry him. Peter approves. After a trial night together Margot and Paul announce their engagement.

NOTES AND GLOSSARY:

Pervigilium Veneris: the title of an anonymous second-century Latin lyric which says: 'tomorrow [he] who has never loved before may fall in love, and [she] who has loved may love again.' This obviously applies to Paul and Margot. The words mean 'Vigil of Venus'

William Morris: poet, artist and idealist (1834–96), a founder of the Society for the Preservation of Ancient Buildings. Waugh uses him as a contrast to Otto Silenus, the ruthless modernist

rather Chokey's taste before: the kind of old English building Chokey enjoyed visiting

Cartier:	a Paris firm of jewellers
The Golden Bough:	the anthropological work by Sir J.G. Frazer (1854–1941), published 1890–1915
Havelock Ellis:	(1859–1939) author of *Studies in the Psychology of Sex* (1897–1910), a work which was banned in England on its first appearance
The Wind in the Willows:	a children's classic (1908) by Kenneth Grahame (1859–1932)
the Coalition:	under Lloyd George (see note to Part One, Chapter VIII) in 1916
the other House:	the House of Lords
Monte:	Monte Carlo, a famous Mediterranean retreat for the rich
a Rag:	high-spirited, violent game
a *rip:*	reckless young man
peerage . . . something quite awful:	as his title; Maltravers later assumes the title Lord Metroland, which Peter considers 'awful'
absinthe frappé:	(*French*) a chilled alcoholic drink

Part Two, Chapter IV Resurrection

Grimes, disguised in a false beard, visits Margot. Paul and Peter waylay him in the drive. He explains that his first wife has turned up; his 'suicide' is no longer credited. An old friend has recommended him for work with Margot Beste-Chetwynde's chain of 'places of entertainment' in South America; he has come to see her about this. Paul produces a letter from Dr Fagan with news from Llanabba: a young Irish woman has been claiming to be Grimes's widow; Prendergast has discovered that a 'Modern Churchman' is allowed to have Doubts and he means to become a clergyman again; the director of a film company, who calls himself Sir Solomon Philbrick, is offering to buy Llanabba Castle.

Potts comes to admire the new house. He shows an interest in Grimes whom he has seen in the drive. He is making enquiries for the League of Nations. Silenus departs.

NOTES AND GLOSSARY:

beaver:	beard
Davy Jones' locker:	the ocean's bottom, where the drowned go, according to sailors
Chanel:	fashionable Paris trademark, created by Gabrielle ('Coco') Chanel (1883–1970) the French couturier responsible for Chanel no 5

to do with the League of Nations: it is already obvious to us, although not to Paul, that Margot is the owner of a chain of brothels in Argentina, and that Potts, in his new job, is investigating her (probably criminal) activities

batik: material with a design printed by a technique using wax

---

Part Two, Chapter V The Latin-American Entertainment Co., Ltd

Peter goes back to Llanabba. Paul and Margot are to be married in London. Margot explains to Paul that there is some South American business to be dealt with before the honeymoon. Margot's business turns out to involve interviewing girls—among them a Jane Grimes—for work in 'entertainment' overseas. Paul is unsuspicious, even when 'someone like Potts' is seen stopping one of Margot's girls in the street. At lunch, in a most expensive restaurant, Paul meets Philbrick, who warns him that the League of Nations is 'getting busy' and that the police may be concerned about Margot's activities. Paul has no idea what he means; but he is used to Philbrick's nonsense.

NOTES AND GLOSSARY:
barbaric: here, old-fashioned
Mendelssohn: Felix Mendelssohn (1809–47); his music is often played at traditional weddings
Mumm: a brand of champagne
the Prince Consort: Prince Albert (1819–61), Queen Victoria's husband
Mr Arlen: Michael Arlen (1895-1956), a popular novelist of the 1920s who depicted life in upper-class London circles ('Mayfair')

Part Two, Chapter VI A Hitch in the Wedding Preparations

Potts declines when Paul invites him to act as best man. Alastair Digby-Vane-Trumpington accepts. There is public excitement about this approaching marriage between schoolmaster and millionairess. Lady Circumference disapproves. (Lord Tangent has recently died.) Paul stays in luxury at the Ritz Hotel surrounded by wedding presents. Margot is to allow him two thousand pounds a year after the wedding.

Some of Margot's girls, on their way to Rio, have been refused permission to sail from Marseilles. Margot asks Paul to fly there and arrange matters. Potts is in the same aeroplane. In the street where the girls are lodged, in the old quarter of Marseilles, Paul is alarmed by the presence of prostitutes, but he still suspects nothing. He is told by the authorities that the League of Nations is now 'making things more difficult'. Finally, the girls are free to sail for South America, and Paul returns to London to be married.

He meets Peter, who has come from school for the wedding, at the Ritz; Llanabba, with new masters, is worse than ever. Presents arrive from the Master of Scone College and from the Argentine legation. Peter and Alastair Trumpington drink champagne. Paul raises his glass to 'Fortune, a much-maligned lady'. Shortly afterwards a policeman arrives with a warrant for Paul's arrest.

NOTES AND GLOSSARY:

Society: upper-class society
Corfu: an island off the Greek coast
Napoleon III: Louis Napoleon Bonaparte (1808–73) became French President in 1848 and later Emperor (1852–1870)
Croydon: formerly the principal civil airport, south of London
bouillabaisse: a fish soup of southern France
Gardez-bien votre chapeau: (*French*) look after your hat!
Pompeii: ancient Roman city near Naples preserved under ashes after a volcanic eruption
Chez Alice: (*French*) Alice's place
Avez-vous les jeunes femmes . . .: (*French*) have you Mrs Beste-Chetwynde's young women here?
Longfellow: Henry Wadsworth Longfellow (1807–82) is perhaps chosen because he wrote 'Poems of Slavery' (1842)

Part Three, Chapter I Stone Walls do not a Prison Make

After the excitement of Paul's arrest there is public disappointment at the dullness of his trial. He is sentenced to seven years' imprisonment with hard labour. Mrs Beste-Chetwynde is not mentioned in court. Peter has visited Paul before the trial to say that if he gives up Margot, Maltravers—now Home Secretary—will marry her and arrange to free Paul. Paul has decided to wait for Margot; but he did not expect such a severe sentence.

In Blackstone Gaol he meets Philbrick, and also Prendergast, who is the prison chaplain. Prendergast is still depressed, for prisoners are just as bad as boys. The prison Governor, Sir Wilfred Lucas-Dockery, is a progressive-minded former sociology professor whose unrealistic plans to improve conditions make him unpopular among the prisoners.

Paul enjoys his first four weeks, spent in solitary confinement. After the responsibilities of his recent life, he finds his cell pleasantly peaceful.

NOTES AND GLOSSARY:

Stone Walls do not . . .: 'Nor Iron Bars a Cage' (the title of Chapter IV in Part Three) is the next line of the lyric 'To Althea from Prison' (1642) by Richard Lovelace (1618-56/7)

Old Bailey: the central criminal court in London where the major court cases of the country are held

Boulestin's: a first-class London restaurant situated in Covent Garden

cat-o'-nine tails: whip

unholy market of humanity: Paul is presumed guilty of 'white slaving'—shipping prostitutes abroad

Oppenheim: E.P. Oppenheim (1866-1946) was a popular writer of stories of mystery and intrigue

Cheltenham Spa: a favourite town for retirement among middle-class people, in the south-west of England

blaspheming against the diction: reading badly from the texts for the service

---

Part Three, Chapter II The Lucas-Dockery Experiments

At the end of his month of solitary confinement, Paul asks for an extension. 'Solitary' is meant to be a punishment. The Governor decides that Paul needs therapy and arranges for him to walk daily in the yard with another prisoner. His first companion is an old hand who provides hints about prison life. Philbrick, Paul discovers, is believed by the prisoners to be the Governor's brother.

Part Three, Chapter III The Death of a Modern Churchman

Paul's next companion for the walks is a former carpenter—a burly lunatic who suffers religious visions and thinks himself 'the lion of the Lord's elect'. He is in prison for having decapitated a 'Philistine'. Paul complains to the Governor, in vain. Sir Wilfred believes the ex-carpenter needs 'therapy' and provides him with a saw. Not long afterwards the madman cuts off Prendergast's head.

NOTES AND GLOSSARY:

Woe unto the Philistine . . .: the view of the Vicar at the Llanabba sports that 'lay interest in ecclesiastical matters is often a prelude to insanity' (Part One, Chapter VIII) seems to be confirmed by this character's behaviour. His speech is full of phrases from the Old Testament. For 'Philistine', see the Bible, 1 Samuel 17

Moabite . . . washpot: see the Bible, Psalms 60:8 and 108:9
whore of Babylon: a term applied by extreme Protestants to the Catholic Church: see the Bible, Revelation 17
'O God, our help in ages past': a hymn by Isaac Watts (1674–1748), under cover of which the prisoners exchange information

---

Part Three, Chapter IV Nor Iron Bars a Cage

Paul is transferred to Egdon Heath Penal Settlement. In the train his warders lend him a newspaper which provides news of Margot and Peter. Peter has succeeded his uncle and is now Earl of Pastmaster. Paul reflects on his own situation. He is taking the blame for Margot, but that seems right; it is impossible to imagine Margot in prison.

Grimes is at Egdon Heath, convicted of bigamy. He left his job in South America when the first Mrs Grimes arrived, and was arrested as soon as he reached England. Dr Fagan's school, it seems, has closed. Paul begins to receive special treatment. The chaplain brings him new novels from a London bookshop; his food contains delicacies; the doctor prescribes him a tonic which turns out to be sherry. Margot writes to him; then she visits him in prison, and is shocked by how he looks. She has—so she tells him—been finding herself socially ostracised. She means to give up her South American business and marry Maltravers.

NOTES AND GLOSSARY:
Low Church: members of the Church of England who disapprove of elaborate ornament and ritual
Radicals: here, reformers who insisted that the law must apply equally to all classes
box: witness box in court
the new Virginia Woolf: Virginia Woolf (1882–1941) published several novels in the 1920s
Smiles's *Self-Help*: *Self Help* (1859) by Samuel Smiles (1812–1904), was written for working men who hoped to better their condition. This—unlike Virginia Woolf— would be standard reading for prisoners
cut: deliberately ignored in public
Tranby Croft: a Victorian scandal in high society which resulted in 'cuts'
Up Jenkins: a children's game
mal soigné: (*French*) badly groomed; unkempt
Alastair . . . rather sweet: Trumpington has replaced Paul as Margot's lover

---

Part Three, Chapter V The Passing of a Public School Man

Grimes tells Paul that he cannot bear prison life: he means to escape. Next day is foggy, and when the prisoners are out at work Grimes seizes one of the warders' horses and makes off across the heath. Later the horse comes back but Grimes is not recaptured. At the end of a week, his hat is found in the mire and he is presumed dead. But Paul reflects, romantically, that Grimes is indestructible: 'one of the immortals'.

NOTES AND GLOSSARY:

Bacchic train: the followers of Dionysus, ancient Greek god of wine and revelry

childish satyrs: satyrs were sensual, semi-human creatures, in Greek mythology

Arcady: ideal country region, in poetry

the Pompeian sentry: he stood at his post while the city was destroyed (see note to Part Two, Chapter VI)

Citadels of the Plain: corrupt ancient cities destroyed by God; see the Bible, Genesis 18–19

the Deluge: Noah's Flood; see Genesis 6–8

when the Darkness . . . : at the Creation, see Genesis 1. Paul's reverie is extended, absurdly, in this pastiche of Romantic prose—perhaps in particular that of Walter Pater (1839–94). See the section on Style in Part 3 of these notes

---

Part Three, Chapter VI The Passing of Paul Pennyfeather

The Governor tells Paul that he is to go to a clinic to have his appendix removed, on an order from the Home Secretary. Paul naïvely objects that this operation has already been performed on him, at school. But, in the prison service, the Home Secretary's orders are final. Paul signs a will leaving all he possesses to Margot. The clinic (by the sea) turns out to be run by Dr Fagan and his daughters. Alastair Digby-Vane-Trumpington is there; he has arranged things. A drunken doctor signs Paul's death-certificate and a statement that he died during the 'operation'. After supper everyone drinks to 'Fortune, a much-maligned lady'. Paul leaves on Margot's steam-yacht, which is waiting in the bay, for her villa in Corfu.

NOTES AND GLOSSARY:

the Home Secretary: Maltravers, who has married Margot on her condition that he will promote the scheme to free Paul which Trumpington carries out

M.D.:	Doctor of Medicine; Dr Fagan adjusts his 'qualifications' to his occupation
Sir Bedivere:	in Arthurian legend he carried King Arthur's body to the barge which bore him to the magic land of Avalon. See *Le Morte Darthur* (*c*.1469) by Sir Thomas Malory (*d*.1471); and 'The Passing of Arthur' (1871) by Alfred Lord Tennyson (1809–92). Like Arthur, Paul has died (in a sense), and is to be born again

Part Three, Chapter VII Resurrection

In Corfu Paul enjoys being 'dead', living quietly and comfortably at Margot's villa. One day he meets Otto Silenus, who has been inspecting Greek remains, without approval. Having no money left, Silenus joins Paul at the Villa. Paul listens to his explanation of what life is like. At Luna Park, in London, there is a revolving wheel: people try to sit on the wheel and are flung off, amusing both them and the spectators. At the centre, the wheel is steadier: there it is possible to stand. Such people as Margot enjoy hanging on at the edge. Silenus is near the centre. But it is not necessary to get on the wheel at all. There are two types of human being, Silenus thinks: the static and the dynamic. Paul is static: he should keep off the wheel!

After some months Paul returns to Scone College. He passes the entrance exams under his old name but with a new identity—and with a large moustache, for disguise. Nobody recognises him and he resumes his old life, studying for the Church. He finds a friend, Stubbs, who is rather like Potts. His adventures have made him cautious; he strongly disapproves of all unorthodoxy.

NOTES AND GLOSSARY:
smalls and Matriculation: university entrance examinations
The Bodleian: the University library at Oxford
Randall Cantuar: the signature of the Archbishop of Canterbury
Jesus: Jesus College
Arnold Bennett: (1867–1931) novelist and writer
there was a bishop: Paul's reading for a theology degree involves studying such heretics of the past. Bithynia was to the south of the Black Sea

Epilogue

It is the evening of the Bollinger Club dinner, in Paul's third year of residence. Stubbs has been taking cocoa with Paul in his college rooms.

They discuss Peter Pastmaster, now at the college, and a Bollinger member. When Stubbs has gone, Peter looks in. He has been drinking heavily. They talk about the past. Paul should never have 'got mixed up with us', Peter says; and Paul agrees: the Beste-Chetwyndes are dynamic; he is static. Peter half recalls the toast 'to Fortune'; then he leaves. Paul settles down to taking notes on early heretics. He disapproves of them all.

NOTES AND GLOSSARY:

Von Hügel: Friedrich Von Hügel (1852–1925); theologian and philosopher

Margot Metroland: Maltravers has taken the title of 'Metroland'. Peter has never liked Maltravers

Quominus **and** *quin:* Latin conjunctions meaning 'lest'; scraps of knowledge recalled from Paul's classes at Llanabba

Part 3

Commentary

Nature, purpose and achievement

Decline and Fall is a satirical novel—light, comic and fantastic. A satire aims to ridicule the vices and follies of its time. The satire of Waugh's 'novelette' is playful and mocking rather than fiercely indignant.

The novel is valued as a comic picture of English society; it is meant to entertain. It is effective as a satire which is meant to disturb the reader and to make him think; it can at times be ominous. *Decline and Fall* is also admired as a skilful work of modern prose. There is a wild, carnival spirit in the book, but every chapter and every sentence is under the writer's control.

Comedy

The chief comic principle is the plight of an earnest, rational young man in a reckless, irrational world. Paul's previous life has been confined to the most respectable, orderly circles; he is now plunged into the most disreputable and disorderly milieux. There are two Englands in *Decline and Fall*: that of Arthur Potts and the chaplain of Scone College; and another which includes Grimes and Margot Beste-Chetwynde. Neither understands the other and when Paul leaves the safety of his old life he becomes a helpless innocent. The gap between his normal expectations and his abnormal adventures is a source of comedy throughout.

Paul himself can be an object of the comedy when we come to feel we understand the 'laws' of his new life better than he does himself. Paul always expects reasonable behaviour and finds the opposite. At the outset, he takes it for granted that he is unqualified for the teaching-post at Llanabba: that, we find, is why Dr Fagan wants to recruit him. At this early stage the reader may be as shocked as Paul is. But at the end of the novel, when Paul protests to his prison Governor that he has already had his appendix removed, he seems absurdly, comically naïve: obviously the caviare in his prison dish, the new novels and glasses of wine mean that Margot and Maltravers are working on his behalf behind the scenes. In the reasonable world Paul still believes in, a Home Secretary —guardian of England's law and order—would not be found plotting a convicted criminal's escape. But by now we have accepted the unreasonable as a rule of the book.

We soon recognise other comic principles. 'To Fortune, a much-maligned lady' is a frequent toast (it could, perhaps, have served as the novel's title). Abrupt, drastic changes occur often enough to seem part of the game. When the story begins, Paul has been at a student meeting, comfortably discussing eastern European politics. He is planning to smoke a pipe and read a chapter of Galsworthy before bed. 'Caught' by the Bollinger, he loses his trousers, and next day everything else: his place at Oxford, his income, his friends, and his future career in the Church. He becomes the colleague of Grimes and Prendergast—failures and outcasts. Within weeks of that downfall, he is engaged to Margot Beste-Chetwynde, is living in the Ritz, and is about to enjoy an allowance of two thousand pounds a year (his salary at Llanabba was ninety); the Master of Scone College sends a wedding-present. Then he is arrested and imprisoned. Before long he is in luxury again, at Margot's villa in Corfu; and, finally, back where he started. Prendergast too has fallen, from his rectory at Worthing into the nightmare of Llanabba; he has further still to fall; a man of 'Doubts', he is slain by a maniacal believer. Grimes is accustomed to changes of fortune. From his unhappy marriage at Llanabba he rises to prosperity in Argentina; then finds himself in prison.

Such reversals supply comic situations, as when Potts explains to Paul at dinner (Part Two, Chapter II) about his 'interesting' new job with the League of Nations, or when Paul meets Philbrick, Prendergast and Grimes in prison. 'You won't find nothing like the Ritz 'ere, you dirty White Slaver,' the warder tells Paul. Waugh observes: 'But there he was wrong, because the next person Paul met was Philbrick' (Part Three, Chapter I).

The turning of Fortune's wheel involves changes of role, another traditional comic device. Fagan's Ph.D. becomes an M.D. and his school a clinic in Part Three. Beste-Chetwynde the schoolboy becomes Peter Pastmaster the Bollinger host. Alastair Digby-Vane-Trumpington helps to cause Paul's downfall at the outset and helps to rescue him at the end. The fraudulent Philbrick lives several roles simultaneously, at least in his own imagination. The wheel of life goes round, Silenus tells Paul, 'and that makes [the world] laugh too' (Part Three, Chapter VII). Characters and situations recur as in a farce. At school Prendergast is ridiculed because he wears a wig. In prison he complains to Paul that 'criminals are just as bad as boys, I find' (Part Three, Chapter I). When Paul is obliged to walk in the yard and make intellectual conversation, as part of the Lucas-Dockery Experiments, the old convict he talks to tells him, 'this blinking prison is going to the dogs. Look at the chaplain. Wears a wig!' (Part Three, Chapter II).

Waugh insists that altered fortunes are not necessarily as good or as bad as we expect. 'People talk a great deal of nonsense about being rich,'

Margot tells Paul. 'But I wouldn't be poor . . . for all the ease in the world' (Part Two, Chapter III). The terms 'rich' and 'poor' are wittily made interchangeable here. In fact, wealth does not suit Paul and he is happier in prison than he was in the Ritz: 'the next four weeks of solitary confinement were among the happiest of Paul's life' (Part Three, Chapter I). This chapter's title is 'Stone Walls do not a Prison Make'; Waugh enjoys the joke that 'anyone who has been to an English public school will always feel comparatively at home in prison' (Part Three, Chapter IV), and he enjoys upsetting the common assumption that prison is harder for the rich than for the poor.

Such comic effects depend on a distance from real feeling. The reader does not share Paul's experiences closely. Paul is often little more than a comic device—'a shadow', Waugh tells us (Part Two, Chapter II). The book would be intolerable if the story had been treated in a realistic manner. As it is, we do not react strongly when Paul is falsely accused, as we do, for example, in *The Last Chronicle of Barset* (1866-7) by Anthony Trollope (1815-82), when Josiah Crawley suffers injustice; there is no aim to stir sympathy or indignation, when Beste-Chetwynde is caned by Prendergast, of the kind we feel when David is caned by Mr Murdstone in Dickens's *David Copperfield* (1850). Prendergast's death is not horrible as certain scenes are in the black comedies of the present-day novelist Angus Wilson (b.1913). In Waugh these are comic events, taking place—we are never meant to forget—in a world of make-believe.

Satire

Waugh's effectiveness as a satirist is in his power to embarrass. He became unpopular, especially in later life, by embarrassing friends and strangers in public. In his fiction his gift for disconcerting is a strength. All forms of pretension, hypocrisy and self-satisfaction are liable to be made self-conscious. Dr Fagan's words to Paul (Part One, Chapter I) come from a character whom it is impossible to take seriously: 'It is vision I need, Mr Pennyfeather, not diplomas'; 'my school is built upon an ideal—an ideal of service and fellowship'; 'Grimes . . . is *not* out of the top drawer, and boys notice these things'. Dr Fagan may be a caricature, but these are the kind of phrases which some real head-masters use; their fatuity is unmistakable here. Potts tells Paul at dinner that he has 'seen some of Silenus's work at Munich'; 'I think that he's a man worth watching' (Part Two, Chapter II). 'I think it's an insult bringing a nigger here,' proclaims Mrs Clutterbuck at the sports; 'it's an insult to our own women' (Part One, Chapter IX). 'I have considered your application with the most minute care,' Sir Wilfred Lucas-Dockery informs Paul. 'In fact I have decided to include it in my forthcoming work on the criminal mind' (Part Three, Chapter II). These voices are lifelike, though the speakers are preposterous. Pomposity, in the knowing undergraduate, racism, in the vulgar woman, the blend of good intentions and personal ambition, in the ineffectual Governor, are especially audible in the farcical contexts Waugh contrives for them.

The comic world of *Decline and Fall* is alive with voices and ideas we know in real life. When we look closely at what the characters say, it becomes harder to distinguish between realism and fantasy in the novel; Waugh has merged them subtly. Dr Fagan's advertisement asks for 'testimonials and photographs, if considered advisable' (Part One, Chapter I). This looks like a comic invention; but Waugh took the phrase from an advertisement for a teaching post which he had answered himself. Grimes seems less implausibly grotesque when we read the author's account of the schoolmaster on whom he was modelled, in the last chapter of *A Little Learning*. The satirical point that Prendergast's doubts are acceptable in 'a Modern Churchman' has become, perhaps, more telling fifty years later. It is a feature of Waugh's satiric art that when the story appears to have moved into pure fantasy, we can be sharply, embarrassingly reminded of contemporary life.

If Waugh had been a reforming satirist with precise targets for attack, his uninhibited comedy might have detracted from the satire. In fact he is clearly not intending to reform Oxford colleges, private schools, or the prison system; he is not attacking the private wealth of Dr Fagan or Margot Beste-Chetwynde. He lampoons everyone: the drunken Bollinger Club members and the sober undergraduates Paul and Potts; Llanabba school and its parents; Lucas-Dockery and his traditional-minded predecessor; Margot's wealth and Prendergast's poverty. The futurist architect Silenus, who prefers machines to people and would like to ignore human needs when designing domestic architecture, is a figure of fun—restless, sleepless, always unsatisfied. But the preservationists who want to save the Tudor King's Thursday are also derided. *Decline and Fall* did not aim at the reform of existing institutions.

Waugh believed that his contemporaries had lost their sense of values, and he wanted to make that loss clear to them in his writing. He is sometimes seen as a forerunner of the twentieth-century writers who have found life meaningless and produced a literature of the Absurd (including 'black', or 'sick' comedy). But such comparisons are misleading: life was not meaningless for Waugh. His conversion to Catholicism was, he declared, a purely rational decision. As a Catholic he was to be a strict believer. He was, as a rationalist and an aesthete, a perfectionist. He admired craftsmanship, in any medium, and expected that to be perfect. He was more acutely aware than most people of all that is irrational and vulgar in society, and inclined to ridicule whatever seemed shoddy, messy or false. An earlier satirist in English—Jonathan

Swift (1667–1745)—suffered from a similar impatience with the irrationality of mankind. (Swift wrote to 'vex' mankind; there is a bitterness in his work which is not present in Waugh's first novel, although he became angrier and more Swiftian later.) While a Swift or a Waugh has nothing constructive to propose which mankind can hope to follow, such satirists make us conscious of the muddled conditions in which we live.

Decline and Fall does not anywhere recommend a moral code. The narrator is non-committal. Vicious characters flourish; the innocent (Tangent and Prendergast) die. But the novel does recommend honesty; it attacks fraudulence of all kinds and at all levels of society (including the Llanabba stationmaster's). The contemporary scene, Waugh asserts, is composed of shams. Llanabba is a sham castle; the school is a pretence; Grimes's status as a 'public-school man' is a joke; the brilliant Mrs Beste-Chetwynde, whom a Cabinet Minister courts, is a criminal; the progressive prison-governor is a fool. The pretensions and fads of the time are turned into a gay, comic masquerade; they are also submitted to a keen scrutiny.

Waugh is like other writers of the 1920s and 1930s in his sense that life in England has gone wrong. Paul and Lord Circumference agree (Part One, Chapter VIII) that another war is due before long. In the meantime, the sad figure of Peter Beste-Chetwynde, drunk and aimless in Paul's rooms at the end of *Decline and Fall*, implies that the England of Dr Fagan and Margot Metroland has little to offer him— or his generation. Waugh's first novel is exuberant but not frivolous.

Craftsmanship

Waugh rightly thought his novels 'well made'. He believed in writing plainly, without literary mannerisms (except for special effects). His comedy and satire depend on the quality of the spare, graceful prose he taught himself. The structure of *Decline and Fall* is equally crafted. His skill in composition made him seem *avant-garde* in 1928; it is still admired today. These aspects of his achievement are considered in detail later, in the sections on Structure and Style.

Background to composition

Decline and Fall is the work of a young man: Waugh was twenty-five in 1928. He had published a story, 'The Balcony', in 1926, and had destroyed one unsuccessful attempt at a novel. Like many first books, *Decline and Fall* is concerned with first experiences of adult life.

Waugh had spent most of his twenty-five years at school or university; the Oxford and Llanabba settings reflect his time as a student and after-

wards as a schoolmaster. Waugh was educated at a good private school
and at a stern but distinguished minor public school where he was very
well taught. In 1925 he began teaching at a private school in Wales. The
independent system of education (in which English boys of Waugh's
social class were usually brought up) can be confusing. Most private
schools, owned by their headmasters, were—though often bizarre—
competently run. Since they were relatively small (even when grandly
housed) and in the control of one man or one family, some could be
'pretty bad', as Mr Levy at Church and Gargoyle's scholastic agency
says of Llanabba. Waugh had been unhappy in Wales, through no fault
of his school; he made Llanabba as bad as possible, creating an absurdly
remote, cynical and avaricious headmaster; inefficient and (in the case
of Grimes and his sadistic successor) perverted members of staff.
Private headmasters have never been allowed to forget *Decline and Fall*,
which depicts too closely for comfort faults to which the worst schools
are liable. Happily such places tend to fail—as Llanabba does.

Public schools (also independent), being larger and run by governors,
with well-qualified staffs, are a different phenomenon. Waugh scoffs at
the social privilege which the major schools (including Eton and
Harrow) conferred, by making the 'common' and unscrupulous Grimes
an old Harrovian, always saved from punishment and disgrace by
being 'a public school man'.

At Oxford Waugh was conscious of the contrast between students
from middle-class homes who worked hard and lived moderately on
their scholarships, and others, often aristocratic or rich, who did little
work and lived recklessly. He came from a middle-class background;
as a history scholar, he was expected to behave sensibly, as Paul is doing
at the outset of *Decline and Fall*. He was attracted by more colourful
circles—by rich and aristocratic, and by bohemian and artistic undergraduate milieux. He lacked the patience to work as Paul does; he also
lacked the money and upper-class social background of Sir Alastair
Digby-Vane-Trumpington. In *Decline and Fall* he satirises both: Paul
as a dull man with his meetings, cocoa and chapter of *The Forsyte Saga*
before bed; Trumpington and Peter Pastmaster as drunken wastrels.

At Oxford and afterwards he had upper-class friends and acquaint-
ances. His first wife, the Honourable Evelyn Gardner (known as 'she-
Evelyn') was a daughter of Lord Burghclere. In London in the 1920s—
when not teaching—he saw 'Mayfair' (high society) at first hand without quite belonging to it: this is Paul's position in Part Two of *Decline
and Fall*. As something of an outsider (his mother-in-law considered
him an 'unsuitable' young man), he was inclined to satirise the bluff,
rural Lady Circumference and the smart, ruthless Margot Beste-
Chetwynde. After the success of his early novels, he became more a part
of upper-class England and more indulgent towards it in his writing.

In 1928 he was equally inclined to ridicule respectable, reliable, middle-class society, which often irked him at home and which he identified with his father. Arthur Waugh was Managing Director of the publishing firm Chapman and Hall, but Evelyn knew that strict professional integrity would prevent his father from publishing work by a member of the family; he also thought his father would disapprove of *Decline and Fall*. Duckworth, the first publishers who were offered the book, refused it. Chapman and Hall accepted it for publication while Arthur Waugh was away. The sexual frankness and general irreverence of the novel was shocking to many reasonable people fifty years ago. The fact that Duckworth objected to the scene in which the Bollinger Club strips Paul of his trousers reminds us of the staid standards of the time and of how refreshingly bold he appeared to those who admired *Decline and Fall* when it first came out.

Structure

The novel's three parts correspond to three settings: Llanabba Castle, Margot's fashionable world, and prison; they are framed by the Oxford scenes of the Prelude and Epilogue. (There are brief interludes while Paul is at his guardian's London house at the start and at Margot's villa on Corfu at the close.) Contrasts and parallels between different stages of Paul's career help to give the novel a strong structure. Oxford is a place of theories, about education (as we see in Potts's letters) and about the world; at Llanabba and afterwards Paul undergoes the squalid realities of school and society. School and prison are compared; Prendergast finds prison as bad as school. Paul takes to it easily, well prepared for austerity by his schooldays. Prison is compared favourably with the luxury of life in Margot's circle; Paul finds it more peaceful.

Metamorphosis is a comic principle throughout (as we have seen) and this contributes to unity. In the dreamlike sequence of Paul's adventures, Potts the friend becomes an accuser; Trumpington the assailant becomes a rescuer; Grimes, Prendergast, Fagan, Philbrick, Silenus and Peter Beste-Chetwynde reappear in new roles as if in a dream—like the creatures in *Alice in Wonderland* (1865) by Lewis Carroll (C.L. Dodgson, 1832–98). A pattern is created by changing fortunes and recurring characters. Otto Silenus's idea of the big wheel at Luna Park as a symbol of life can be linked with the characters' favourite toast of 'Fortune, a much-maligned lady'; Fortune traditionally turns her wheel. We finish the novel with the sense of a circle completed when Paul returns to his starting point (and the next Bollinger dinner takes place). *Decline and Fall* is a highly patterned novel.

Waugh's ingenious handling of a limited cast of characters, all fully employed, might remind us of dramatic comedy. The novel has the logical control of absurd events and the careful plotting we find in farce. The story prepares us for coming events. The sports make a fine display of Llanabba Castle school's deficiencies; they also introduce Paul to Margot. An interest in the League of Nations is just what we should expect of Paul and Potts as undergraduates: it leads to Paul's arrest and conviction on Potts's evidence. Mrs Grimes's application for a South American job shows us Margot's recruiting methods (Part Two, Chapter V); her arrival in Argentina provokes Grimes's return to England and imprisonment at Egdon Heath. Paul can only escape from prison by 'dying'; his 'death' allows him (given the licence of comedy) to return to Scone. The story is tightly organised.

The swift changes of scene are managed deftly, without cumbersome explanations. Much of the action is dramatic; dialogue often conveys the necessary details of what is happening; others are given incidentally. Lord Tangent's fate is a good example of how economic Waugh can be: 'Tangent's foot has swollen up and turned black,' Beste-Chetwynde tells Paul 'with relish' during an organ lesson (Part One, Chapter XII). Everyone at Llanabba attends Grimes's wedding, we are told (Part One, Chapter XIII), except Dr Fagan and 'little Lord Tangent, whose foot was being amputated at a local nursing-home'. 'It's maddenin' Tangent having died just at this time,' says Lady Circumference (Part Two, Chapter VI)—because people may imagine that to be her reason for avoiding Margot's wedding. The macabre shock is increased by the indirect, casual reporting. Occasionally Waugh indulges in a set-piece, such as Fagan's diatribe against the Welsh (Part One, Chapter VIII), or the account of the old King's Thursday (Part Two, Chapter I). More often, he builds up effects with a series of inconspicuous details. The forms and colours of the newly rebuilt King's Thursday are revealed gradually in the course of Paul's story. In constructing *Decline and Fall*, Waugh worked hard to make the reading easy.

The scenes are connected with interspersed passages of narrative and comment in which we grow familiar with the detached voice of the story-teller. Quietly and politely, he keeps us informed, never obtruding or causing a sense of delay. There is a deliberate contrast between the narrator's cool control and the wild goings-on. Events are more amusing because so drily described. The story's extravagance makes the disciplined prose pleasing. Waugh's style contributes to the novel's structure and unity.

Style

The writing is fluent and precise. Words are not wasted; we soon recognise that they are carefully used.

Waugh is laconic. His comments are reserved. 'It was a lovely evening,' he writes in the Prelude, and goes on to describe the damage to students' rooms as the Bollinger Club rampages through Scone College. Dickens or Thackeray, dealing with such a scene, would have been more heavily sarcastic. Waugh refuses to be obvious; he lets the word 'lovely', joined to the vandalism, speak for itself. 'Clearly the social balance was delicately poised,' he comments on the comedy of manners where Lady Circumference confronts the Clutterbucks (Part One, Chapter IX). This social occasion, in the tent at the sports, is so far from delicate that the word 'delicately' is disdainful—but no disapproval is expressed. Sometimes Waugh makes a value-word seem neutral, almost a technical term: 'ten men of revolting appearance were approaching' (Part One, Chapter VIII). Another writer describing the Llanabba silver band might have said that they appeared revolting to Paul. Waugh's objectivity makes the word pungent. Exaggeration contributes to the comedy, here and elsewhere: *all ten* are revolting. The detach-ment of the writing reinforces the humour. Elsewhere it gives a similar force to a word of disapproval: Margot's career is said to have been 'eventful and in many ways disgraceful' (Part Two, Chapter I). 'Dis-graceful' is more effective because unexpected and without fuss. The narrator has the type of authority which comes from never raising the voice.

The narrative style is briskly efficient; it carries the story along so well that a careless reader might fail to notice how well it is done. Sometimes the romantic impulse in Waugh shows briefly, often stirred by thoughts of the past. When Paul is in the back streets of Marseilles, we are told he has 'traversed the forsaken streets of Pompeii'—a more evocative way of saying he has visited the Roman remains at Pompeii on holiday. After Grimes's escape from prison and disappearance on the heath, he is presumed dead. Paul does not believe it: 'surely he had followed in the Bacchic train of distant Arcady . . .' (Part Three, Chapter V). In that paragraph Waugh is imitating the rhythmic sentences and poetic diction of certain nineteenth-century prose writers whose mannerisms he nor-mally avoids: we are meant to see this 'purple passage' as a parody. But Waugh liked to use 'purple' (affected, elevated) prose occasionally: there are such passages in all his books.

Waugh's descriptions are precise and vivid. He is keenly aware of architecture, décor and costume. The mock-Gothic buildings at Llan-abba are pictured in detail; so is the interior of the Hotel Metropole (Part One, Chapter XII). Mrs Beste-Chetwynde first appears (Part One, Chapter VIII) with 'two lizard-skin feet, silk legs, chinchilla body' and a tiny black hat. Beste-Chetwynde has a Charvat dressing-gown; throughout, Waugh specifies trade-names and makes of jewellery, per-fume or motor cars. This care with details gives a contemporary realism to his sometimes implausible scenes.

Much of the novel's fun is in the dialogue. Waugh is good at catching different dialects and registers. The Llanabba sports provide examples of how these can be mingled: the orotund Dr Fagan lectures Paul on the Welsh in the rapid style of a lecturer who has said it all before. Flossie, chattering about her frock, and Lady Circumference, crisply confident, are characterised by tricks of speech: Flossie by vulgar idioms—'what' instead of 'which', and the repetitive 'does'; Lady Circumference by '-in'' for '-ing' ('shockin' bad'), an old-fashioned upper-class speech habit. The ungentlemanly Grimes uses breezy military slang. The Welsh stationmaster speaks in convoluted, breathless sentences—Waugh's impression of Welsh English. Mrs Beste-Chetwynde has the latest slang of smart society: 'too boring'; 'too shattering'. The variety of English reflects the rich gathering of social types.

Characterisation

The characters are contrived to serve Waugh's comic and satirical purposes; they have no depth and do not seem real enough to arouse much sympathy or concern. They are caricatures of social types, vivid, funny, and memorable. Names are either whimsical (Tangent, Circumference) or typical (the plain Potts in contrast to the noble Digby-Vane-Trumpington). Major characters tend to have more than one role. Waugh's inventiveness produces a large cast of background figures who appear only briefly but are lively and distinct.

Paul Pennyfeather

The 'real' Paul Pennyfeather is described (Part Two, Chapter II) as a responsible, able, cultured, handsome young man. He is almost the ideal product of an old-fashioned, middle-class upbringing: cautious, conservative, and reliable.

After his expulsion from Scone, Waugh tells us, this solid young man becomes 'a shadow'; in other words, he is a caricature suited to the fanciful story. The name Pennyfeather suggests lightness and lack of substance. His role requires him to be passive: he accepts expulsion, banishment to Llanabba and prison without protest. His naïvety is exaggerated for the sake of the plot and the humour; we sense this most strongly when he arranges the shipping of Margot's girls from Marseilles to Rio without grasping the nature of the Latin American Entertainment Company. Although innocent, Paul is not a fool. He adapts to his job at Llanabba and to prison. He shows unexpected firmness at times—as on his first morning in the classroom. He has a sense of fun, which helps him to adapt; remembering Dr Fagan's advice that schoolmasters' need to 'temper discretion with deceit', the unmusical Paul tells Beste-Chetwynde that he gave organ lessons to the Master of Scone (Part One, Chapter III).

Paul is prepared to be sociable, but he prefers peace and quiet. Friendly, patient, and sympathetic, fastidious, reticent, honourable and polite, he is a contrast to almost everyone he meets. Otto Silenus tells him that people are of two kinds: static and dynamic. Paul is static, and at the end he resolves to live accordingly. When we leave him he is less tolerant than before, reproaching Peter for drunkenness, and disapproving of all heresy. He will make an excellent parson.

Margot Beste-Chetwynde

Beautiful, beautifully dressed, her scent 'almost unprocurable', she arrives at Llanabba like a breath of spring air. Waugh gives her every attribute of the rich, cosmopolitan, independent woman of fashion and in her depicts fashionable crazes of the time. (Jazz music and Africana were popular; the young man she brings to the sports is a black American.) Margot is charming but ruthless. She can be reckless with money, rebuilding King's Thursday twice, but she is a shrewd businesswoman. She assumes a manner of languid indifference, though her toughness appears in the scene where she interviews girls (Part Two, Chapter V).

To Paul, to Maltravers, and to her son, she is the most wonderful woman in the world. They cannot imagine her in prison; Paul is prepared to serve seven years on her behalf; Maltravers breaks the law (in freeing Paul) in order to marry her. Lady Circumference dislikes and disapproves of her, because Margot is richer than the Circumferences and because her behaviour is scandalous. Without a husband (she is rumoured to have poisoned him) and with a succession of young men (Trumpington succeeds Paul), Margot is 'talked about'. The greater potential scandal of her Latin American 'company' is kept a secret, but after Paul's imprisonment she finds herself ostracised and marries Maltravers (now Lord Metroland) to protect her reputation. She is unscrupulous, decisive, elegant and gay; 'there is no one like her', as Maltravers tells Paul (Part Two, Chapter III).

Dr Fagan

Augustus Fagan, Ph.D. (later 'M.D.') is a gentlemanlike rogue. He is very old and very well-dressed. He values Paul as a gentleman (but pays him as little as possible) and regrets that Grimes is not a gentleman—Fagan could forgive him anything else. His daughters are not ladies and he suffers this, with some detachment. He keeps up appearances at Llanabba on the meanest budget, making three thousand pounds a year from the school (the masters are each paid about a hundred a year). Whether or not his doctorate is genuine, he is a cultured man. His moments of frankness are often funny. He is enterprising on an ambitious scale; his clinic, at the end of the novel, is grandiose, though dilapidated. At Llanabba he is headmasterly in speech and in foibles—including exaggerated respect for rich and titled parents, and for 'tone'. Waugh had endured several headmasters as employers; he must have enjoyed creating Dr Fagan.

The name is likely to recall Dickens's Fagin, who keeps a school of boy pickpockets in *Oliver Twist* (1837). But Waugh often (mischievously) used the names of real people for disreputable characters; there was a theatre-manager named Fagan at Oxford.

Captain Grimes

Some of Grimes's characteristics were suggested to Waugh by the conduct of a former colleague whose sexual abuse of boys is described in the final chapter of *A Little Learning*. Grimes has always been in trouble: he was expelled from Harrow School and is now dismissed at termly intervals from the schools in which he teaches. Only his prestige as a 'public school man' preserves him, as it did from court-martial and firing squad, in the army, where the major sent to try his case decided 'we can't shoot an old Harrovian' (Part One, Chapter III). Waugh ridicules this supposedly superior caste (he had been to a minor public school) by making Grimes a sordid figure: he rarely has a bath; he is 'not a gentleman'. His wooden leg, his grotesque appearance and his slang are offensive to many of the characters—though not to Flossie. The necessity of marrying her depresses him, but for most of the novel he is engagingly cheerful. Grimes is a pagan figure who likes drink and company and lives for pleasure. He describes the position of beer-taster which Mr Clutterbuck offers him as 'God's own job' (Part One, Chapter XIII). He cannot endure imprisonment. Paul, at the end, thinks of him as an 'immortal' who has survived from some remote past period. Waugh treats Grimes's vice as a joke. Clutterbuck is apparently fond of him.

Mr Prendergast

The shabby-genteel, unhappy, ineffectual schoolmaster who once knew better days is a common figure in fiction. Prendergast cannot control his pupils; he is mercilessly ragged. His collection of pipes is his only consolation. His only hope is that his religious doubts will end; then he will go back to the comfortable clergyman's life he left ten years ago. When he has one glass of whisky with Grimes on Sports Day it makes him drunk; further roused by champagne in the refreshment tent, he takes his revenge on the boys in the evening. Paul's dinner-party at the Hotel Metropole is his only other satisfaction in the novel. When, still doubting, he becomes a 'Modern Churchman', he finds life as a prison chaplain no easier than school. With his cheap wig and plaintive manner, his childish innocence, his futile life and gruesome death, he would be a pathetic figure if we took him more seriously. As it is, Mr Prendergast provides Waugh with a rich source of jokes.

Philbrick

The school butler gives Paul and his colleagues various fantastic accounts of his past life, none of which (he admits) is true. In fact, he has often been in prison and the police are pursuing him now. His practice is to play the part of a rich man ('Sir Solomon Philbrick') at large hotels and so obtain credit and cash cheques. He seems half to believe in his own fantasies, and is generally cheerful, with a liking for bizarre clothes. Like Grimes, he is incorrigible. He is last seen driving through Oxford in a Rolls Royce car. In a world of shams, it is implied, he is one more false pretender: Margot, Fagan and Lucas Dockery are frauds too. Some readers find his tall stories the least entertaining parts of the novel.

Flossie and Dingy

Florence (Flossie) Fagan is a comic contrast to her imposing father: she dresses luridly and speaks in vulgar, uneducated English. Her sister Diana (known in the school as Dingy) is drabber and obsessed with economies. Both sisters are reminiscent of Dickens; Dingy's thrift recalls that of the Squeers family who keep a squalid private school in Dickens's *Nicholas Nickleby* (1839). Flossie remains with her father after Grimes's disappearance; the sisters are nurses in his clinic at the end of the story.

Lady Circumference

The Countess of Circumference is based on the kind of country gentlewoman who hunts and attends to the farms on her husband's estates. She is dominating; her husband is a pale figure beside her. She has tough views on education: her son Tangent needs 'beatin''; her nephew Trumpington should have had the 'nonsense' knocked out of him when younger. She is combative, furious when Clutterbuck cheats in the three-mile race, and quick to quarrel with the (socially inferior) Clutterbuck family. She resents and later seeks to censure Margot. She is a formidable woman.

Arthur Potts

Potts is needed for the plot: he corresponds with Paul from Oxford, telling him of Alastair Trumpington's offer of twenty-pounds, and he collects the evidence in Marseilles which convicts Paul. He is given the intellectual interests of a serious-minded undergraduate: Waugh treats his style and manner satirically.

Sir Alastair Digby-Vane-Trumpington

Trumpington, a Bollinger Club member, represents upper-class under-graduate life—as Waugh presents it—at Oxford. He is an idle, worldly contrast to the hard-working, naïve, middle-class Paul, whom he supplants as Margot's lover. He very competently arranges the hiring of an alcoholic doctor to sign Paul's death certificate.

Otto Silenus

'Professor' Silenus (who is scarcely twenty-five) has a reputation as an architect of the newest kind. Waugh creates, in him and his work, a comic version of the architectural movement associated with the Bauhaus in Germany (see Notes and Glossary to Part Two, Chapter II above) and with the architect Walter Gropius (1883–1969). Silenus, coldly inhuman himself, despises the busy, messy lives of human beings, preferring the clean efficiency of machines. He dislikes all the architecture of the past, including that of Greece. He elaborates the ideas of life as a wheel and of dynamic and static types of people when he meets Paul there at the end.

Sir Humphrey Maltravers

Maltravers is Minister of Transportation when Paul meets him. Later he becomes Home Secretary and a peer (Lord Metroland). Margot and Peter despise him because he is a bore and because he has risen (as he explains at length to Paul) from humble social origins. He is an amusing contrast to the younger members of the houseparty at King's Thursday (whom he cheats at cards). He is equally unscrupulous as Home Secretary, agreeing to arrange Paul's escape. Waugh continued to ridicule Maltravers, and other political characters, in later books.

Sir Wilfred Lucas-Dockery

A former sociology professor, he is using his position as Prison Governor to make an academic reputation by conducting penal 'experiments'. Waugh ridicules these. Lucas-Dockery has no real knowledge of his prisoners and his conception of criminal derangement is superficial. After Prendergast's death, he confines himself to studying statistics and the prison reverts to the old (presumably venomous) methods of his predecessor, Colonel MacAdder.

Peter Beste-Chetwynde

Peter, who is fifteen at the beginning of the story, is childish in some respects, precocious in others. He schemes to avoid gym and reads *The Wind in the Willows*. His other favourite book is a work on sexual psychology; he drinks heavily at home. Socially self-confident (and snobbish), he befriends Paul and takes charge of him. When Paul meets him at Oxford four years later, he is—as Lord Pastmaster—bored by life, perhaps because he has seen too much of it too soon.

Minor characters

Paul's guardian is typical of fathers in Waugh's novels: he is mean and lacking in sympathy. He is one of many marginal characters: Mr Levy at the scholastic agency ('it's wonderful what one can teach when one tries'; Part One, Chapter I); Chokey (Mr Sebastian Cholmondley), who exists for the sake of the satire in Part One, Chapter IX; the Llanabba stationmaster, Waugh's caricature of a Welshman; Miles Malpractice, the homosexual; his friend David Lennox, who makes an *avant-garde* photographic study of the back of Margot's head; the seemingly meek first Mrs Grimes, who drives Grimes from South America; Clutterbuck the 'nasty little boy', and the doomed Tangent; and the religious maniac in prison who describes his visions to Paul (Part Three, Chapter III) and afterwards saws off Prendergast's head as a sign to Israel. In the background are dons, schoolboys, parents, prostitutes, warders, prisoners, doctors, chaplains and undergraduates. Even very minor figures are often given good lines: Sniggs, the Junior Dean (on the first page): 'please God, make them attack the Chapel'; and the old burglar (in Part Three, Chapter IV) who is given Paul's caviare by mistake, and protests at this irregularity: 'And on bacon night, too!'

Part 4

Hints for study

Study topics

These topics are related to the earlier parts of the notes.

Introduction

(1) How did Waugh's upbringing, followed by his unsettled years after university, influence his view of English society?
(2) Why did Waugh's reputation change after 1945?
(3) Why do critics disagree about Waugh?
(4) Why did he choose the title of *Decline and Fall*?
(5) Which earlier writers influenced him and why?
(6) Why did he like to think of himself as a 'craftsman'?
(7) What was his attitude to nineteenth-century literature?
(8) What was new in his approach to writing fiction?

Summaries

(1) List the main incidents of the novel in order.
(2) Make a list of scenes, (a) involving two people, (b) involving a group of people. Comment on Paul's behaviour in scenes (a) and (b).
(3) Trace the course of Paul's involvement with the Beste-Chetwynde circle.
(4) Trace the course of Paul's relationship with Margot.
(5) Make a list of turning-points in the story. Show what happens as a result in each case.
(6) Make a list of scenes in which Waugh prepares us for later events (for example, Peter's visit to Paul before his trial).
(7) Summarise in your own words some of the major scenes: the Bollinger dinner; the Sports; Paul's visit to King's Thursday, and so on.

Commentary

Nature, purpose and achievement
(1) What is Paul's role in the comedy?
(2) How does Waugh use changes of fortune for comic effect?
(3) What are the other comic devices?

(4) How does Waugh make comedy out of misfortunes and disasters?
(5) To what extent is the novel a fantasy?
(6) To what extent is it realistic?
(7) To what extent is the satire traditional?
(8) What is original in Waugh's satire?
(9) Is Waugh a moralist?
(10) What is Waugh attacking in the English society of the 1920s?

Background to composition
(1) What kind of school is Llanabba meant to represent?
(2) What was Waugh's experience of schools?
(3) What was his attitude to upper-class society?
(4) Why did he have difficulty in publishing *Decline and Fall*?

Structure
(1) Why is the novel set out in three parts with a Prelude and an Epilogue?
(2) What kinds of pattern can be found in *Decline and Fall*?
(3) How does Waugh organise his group of characters?
(4) How does he organise the plot?
(5) What use does he make of contrast?
(6) What is the significance of Silenus's idea of life as a great wheel in a fun-fair?
(7) How does the style contribute to the structure?

Style
(1) What does 'laconic' mean?
(2) Find examples of wording which is surprising and appropriate.
(3) What makes good dialogue?
(4) If you were given passages of dialogue without the characters' names, could you identify them? Test yourself.
(5) Find examples of good descriptive writing in *Decline and Fall*.
(6) Study Waugh's use of detail in describing: clothes; buildings; interiors; people.

Characterisation
(1) Contrast, point by point:
>   Paul and Alastair Trumpington
>   Grimes and Prendergast
>   Fagan and Flossie
>   Flossie and Dingy
>   Lady Circumference and Margot
>   Paul and Silenus
>   Paul and Margot

(2) Compare, point by point:
>
> Paul and Potts
>
> Peter and Margot
>
> Peter and Alastair
>
> 'static' characters
>
> 'dynamic' characters

(3) Imagine that you are to advise the actors in a dramatised version of *Decline and Fall*. What advice would you give to the player of each part?

(4) Which scenes would you choose to illustrate each character's particular personality? Give reasons for your choice.

(5) Does Waugh try to influence the way the reader thinks about the characters?

(6) How do Waugh's characters differ from characters in other novels you know well?

(7) What does it mean to say that a novel's characters are 'caricatures'?

(8) Are Waugh's characters distinct from one another? Are we likely to confuse any of them? Are we likely to remember them long after reading the novel?

Patterns and themes

Here are some groups of topics and points on which to concentrate:

Themes

> 'Fortune, a much maligned lady'

Money	Contentment
Freedom	Confinement
Injustice	Deception
Scandal	Prestige
Social Status	Misleading appearances
'Static' life	'Dynamic' life

Motifs

Drink and drunkenness	Architecture
Changes of role	Novelty and fashion
Theology and 'doubts'	Confessions and life-stories

Settings

Oxford	Llanabba
London	Wales
School	Prison
High society	Low society
the old King's Thursday	Silenus's King's Thursday

Quotations

Students should form the habit of finding apt quotations for use in essays and examination answers. Brief quotations from *Decline and Fall* appear in all sections of Part 3 of these notes. Look for others, and be careful to study the context in which the words appear. Comments often reveal the speaker. Look for short quotations with many implications. 'I am concerned with "style",' remarks Dr Fagan (Part One, Chapter VIII). He has no equipment for the sports and thinks that a starting-pistol would create 'style': the false impression of a proper Sports Day. These words could provide a key to Dr Fagan; they could be applied to other characters who live in style (Philbrick, Margot), or to the novel's treatment of fraud as an object of satire. Alternatively, the same words could illustrate dramatic irony: Prendergast's shooting of Tangent with Philbrick's pistol is to be the least stylish incident of the sports.

Here are a few quotations from Waugh's autobiographical volume *A Little Learning*, Chapman and Hall, London, 1964. Consider how each quotation can be related to *Decline and Fall*, and how the novel draws on Waugh's personal experience.

On style
'But I do not regret my superficial classical studies in Latin and Greek. I believe that the conventional defence of them is valid; that only by them can a boy fully understand that a sentence is a logical construction and that words have basic inalienable meanings . . . .' (p.139)

On school
'Assistant masters came and went [at the private school Waugh attended as a child in Hampstead]. By no means all of them had university degrees . . . . Then and for many years later prep-school masters were drawn from a heterogeneous and undefinable underworld into which—little did I know it—I was myself destined to descend.' (p.84)

On Oxford
'From the first I regarded Oxford as a place to be inhabited and enjoyed for itself . . . . At Oxford I was reborn in full youth. My absurdities were those of exuberance and naivety . . . I wanted to do everything and know everyone . . . .' (p.171)

On teaching
'. . . as the scholastic agent remarked, few headmasters were able to find men with all the qualities they demanded, and with desperate levity I offered to teach anything . . .' (p.215)

'Once my [teaching] colleagues and I went to dinner at the big hotel in Llandudno . . . and I fell into a melancholy . . . seeing myself as Comus Bassington [in Saki's novel *The Unbearable Bassington*; see 'Literary background' in Part 1 of the notes] . . . . Thus the weeks [of teaching] passed in deep self-pity.' (p.226)

On the original 'Grimes'
'Every disgrace had fallen on this irrepressible man, at school, at the university, in the army, and . . . as schoolmaster; disgraces such as, one was told, make a man change his name and fly the kingdom . . .' (p.229)

Arranging material

Two hints should always be kept in mind: to distinguish between the essential and the incidental; and to view the novel as a whole (its overall design and meaning), whatever topic is undertaken in an essay or answer.

Suppose, for example, you are writing about the character of Paul. Such details as his being an orphan or his good looks can be kept in reserve: do not start with these. Look for some idea about him which will allow you to organise your essay: you might want to take Otto Silenus's idea that Paul is a 'static' person who has been living among 'dynamic' friends. This is one way of regarding him and it provides a method for proceeding. His 'normal' life at Oxford can be described to establish that he is a quiet, earnest, studious, unadventurous young man: he has only four friends and three of these were at school with him; he is careful to live within the income from his scholarships and allowance; he smokes and drinks, but very moderately; he attends discussions on serious subjects and goes to bed early; he has never heard of the Bollinger Club. We can say how unlike Waugh's behaviour at Oxford all this is, and point out that Waugh is depicting a model student of the settled, 'static' kind; Paul is introduced not as an individual but as a type we are meant to recognise. The scene in which he is 'caught' by the Bollinger Club requires the contrast between Paul's ideally 'static' student characteristics and the aggressive 'dynamism' of the Bollinger members.

Developing this idea, we can consider his time at Llanabba as the experience of a 'static' man among more 'dynamic' associates. He is at a loss in the classroom, confronted by the turbulence of the boys, until aided by the vigorous Captain Grimes. He adjusts to his new surroundings by arranging a truce with his pupils, but the prospect of Sports Day alarms him. Philbrick's tall stories of a dynamic life of crime appal him.

We could go on to discuss his relationship with Margot in the same terms. She is the most dynamic character of all, as Silenus says: she loves danger; she hangs on to the edge of the revolving wheel of life. When Paul tries to live dynamically (flying to Marseilles to arrange the shipping of Margot's girls), disaster follows. Paul's imprisonment is a relief to him—even solitary confinement is enjoyable—because it is a return to stability.

Here you have a brief illustration (which could be filled out and extended) of how a straightforward topic can be managed. First, look for what seems to you to be essential in the question set: perhaps that the novel is dramatic, or that it is a 'black comedy' or that the satire is aimed at false pretences. Follow your own judgement, and try to apply it to the requirements of the question, choosing an idea which will connect the incidental points you want to make.

In using detail, try to make each point serve a purpose. Quotations should be used to illustrate points. Do not make excessive use of quotation, though, and do not quote just for the sake of it.

Look for comparisons with other books you are studying. There must be a point to such comparisons and you must make that clear. Do not digress.

Specimen questions

Questions could be set on all the topics treated in Part 3, 'Commentary'. Students should look carefully at the precise wording of a question.

Major topics
  (1) '*Decline and Fall* is comic but sad.' Do you agree?
  (2) Illustrate Waugh's handling of dramatic scenes.
  (3) Show how Waugh's use of language contributes to the comedy.
  (4) Show how Paul is contrasted to other characters and explain why.
  (5) Write on the novel's settings.
  (6) Discuss Waugh's treatment of dialogue, *or* description, *or* story-telling, *or* characterisation.
  (7) Does the novel create a full and convincing picture of a social world?
  (8) Write on Waugh's treatment of education.
  (9) Write on Waugh as a satirist.
 (10) How effective is the ending of the novel?

Minor topics
  (1) Write on one of the following: possessions, children, architecture, love, scandal, in *Decline and Fall*.
  (2) Is religious belief treated seriously?
  (3) What is the role of Silenus?

(4) What is the role of Philbrick?

(5) What is Waugh's attitude to Sir Wilfred Lucas-Dockery?

Specimen answers

Major topics

(1) *'Decline and Fall* is comic but sad.' Do you agree?

Many novelists, given the plot of *Decline and Fall*, would have produced a depressing book. Thomas Hardy, for example, treats misfortunes in a very different spirit. Like Hardy, Waugh found life painful. But this is the novel of a young man, who delights in his own comic inventiveness and views the world of his time with a satirist's detachment. There is no place for sadness, except perhaps at the very end.

The story is a series of disasters in which guilty and innocent characters are equally affected. Paul is expelled from Oxford in disgrace; later, when his fortunes are about to be restored, he loses Margot and goes to prison. Prendergast has fallen from comfort and respect in his Worthing rectory to poverty and daily humiliation at Llanabba; his fate as prison chaplain is worse. Captain Grimes brings troubles on himself. Almost all the characters suffer in some way. Fagan's school closes; Margot has to marry Maltravers; Philbrick goes to prison; Tangent dies; Flossie and Dingy fail to find husbands; Mrs Grimes and the madman who kills Prendergast are wretched figures. The novel concentrates on excessive behaviour—on drunkenness, destruction and perversion. The mild Paul enters a frenzied, terrible world.

Waugh intends to stress the random and unjust aspects of life, and of English society. But he presents his story in such a way that the reader is protected from feeling sympathy or sorrow. We are distanced from events. We are not allowed to feel that the victims are real enough to be pathetic; Waugh intervenes to tell us (in Part Two, Chapter II) that the Paul of the novel is only a shadow. After a superficial reading it might be said that *Decline and Fall* is composed of comic anecdotes. It does seem to claim the licence of anecdotes, which we do not allow to trouble us when the joke is past; clearly, many incidents can be extracted and told as 'good stories'.

There is, however, a different kind of aesthetic pleasure when we recognise the author's ingenuity in plotting the movements of his characters: the novel is highly organised. The comic vision is consistent: it is tough and intellectual because satirical. The vices and follies of the time are derided (as the title might lead us to expect). At Oxford and at Llanabba, in high society and in prison, we find false pretences—a world of liars and frauds.

W.M. Thackeray's *Vanity Fair* was a satirical novel which came to the same conclusion about England in 1848. *Vanity Fair* is comic, but pervaded by sadness; it saddened its author, and Thackeray mellowed in later books. Readers who know this larger, Victorian 'Decline and Fall' will see by comparison how free from melancholy Waugh's book is. Writers of the 1920s were in revolt against the Victorians and especially against their sentimentality. The horrors of the First World War had hardened the literary world. After suffering on such a scale, Waugh and his contemporaries felt, private misfortunes were better treated in a comic spirit. Satire should have a cutting edge.

Some readers will find the last scene graver and sadder than the rest. The intoxicated Peter is not treated as the joke Alastair Trumpington is in the Prelude. Peter is rich, young, and a peer; but he drinks too much, he says, because there is nothing else to do. At the close, Waugh allows a moment of pathos to his picture of England in 1928. Peter cannot recall the words of the novel's toast to 'Fortune, a much-maligned lady'. But the book ends on a stern note as Paul reads about ancient heretics. 'Quite right to suppress them.' The hint of melancholy is briskly dispelled.

---

(2) Illustrate Waugh's handling of dramatic scenes.

Waugh confined himself to his chosen craft of prose narrative: after leaving school, he never wrote plays. But *Decline and Fall* shows the skill he might have brought to writing drama. In reading many of the best scenes, we can see—as in reading Dickens—how well they would work if adapted for the stage.

The Prelude begins with two Oxford dons sheltering from a party of riotous students and former students. As they watch, they describe what is happening 'off-stage'. We might have expected them to be shocked or anxious: in fact they are gloating at the prospect of rich fines tomorrow and the best college port in celebration. The noise of shouting and smashing in the background makes a dramatic contrast to their glee. When the innocent figure of Paul Pennyfeather appears, coming home for a quiet read before bed, we can guess what is going to happen. He meets the Bollinger diners; Lumsden, Laird of Strathdrummond, lurches up to him and seizes his tie. (In a stage version we should see that it has the Bollinger colours.) Paul and his captors disappear from our view but the onlooking dons keep us informed: it is only Pennyfeather! How many clothes he has lost! But he is 'of no importance'! In the text, the Bollinger Club and their victim are described by the narrator. But the essential effects arise from the dramatic contrasts: between the dons and the diners; between the sober Paul and the drunken Laird. Waugh's presentation through the dialogue of two onlookers would work equally well in a play.

As the story continues, scenes are contrasted: the calm moral dis-approval of the college meeting which condemns Paul follows the noise and the callousness of the opening. Paul's prosperous guardian, who tells him that he must now face life 'in the raw' (lighting a cigar as he says so), is succeeded by the shabby setting of the scholastic agency. Here the unworldly, youthful Paul is recruited by the worldly, aged Dr Fagan. Their conversation is good drama: Paul meekly admits that he has no experience of teaching; the headmaster cheerfully welcomes the fact. The element of surprise for the reader in Dr Fagan's reactions might remind us of scenes in the plays of Oscar Wilde. In Waugh and in Wilde, normal values are turned upside down; Waugh may have been influenced by the wit and paradox of Wilde.

The classroom scene at Llanabba is an example of a strong dramatic entry altering the balance of events: in this case, the balance of power between Paul and his pupils. The boys await him 'bright with expecta-tion': they mean to stage a comedy. There is a chorus of 'good-morning sir', and a chorus of 'Tangent' when they all claim to the title. Paul's attempt to sort things out fails; he shouts for silence; becomes embar-rassed by the silence; and soon loses control. The boys are fighting when Grimes comes in. Then there is quiet. Grimes gives Paul his stick and leaves. Now we have a tense moment: Paul's position depends on what he does as he faces his form. It is not the stick but his decisiveness that wins. He sets an essay—on self-indulgence—with a prize for the *longest*. The form submits. This is a funny and convincing classroom drama. It depends on the author's sense of timing: Grimes's abrupt entry and exit and his dramatic presentation of the stick create a lull which gives Paul his chance, and he acts fast. In a few moments the helpless master has become masterful; we feel Paul's sense of relief.

In the two chapters which deal with Sports Day at Llanabba, Waugh presents a crowded scene with a rich variety of social types. The domin-eering figure of Lady Circumference, furious with the Clutterbucks about the three-mile race, is checked by the cool superiority of Margot Beste-Chetwynde, whose arrival is another example of a good stage-entry. In the background is the pathetic figure of the injured Tangent, the absurd figure of Prendergast drunk, with his wig awry, and the incongruous presence of a silver band. In the foreground the guests grumble about Margot's companion Chokey: he dominates them, none the less, with serene self-assurance and fluent talk. Throughout the comic sequence of the sports there is impending catastrophe, constantly and narrowly averted. This is good drama, adroitly handled.

Some scenes are comedy of a traditional type. Paul's arrest on his wedding day, as Peter Beste-Chetwynde and Alastair Trumpington drink champagne and Paul (ironically) toasts 'Fortune, a much-maligned lady', is a dramatic interruption of events of a kind familiar to us from the theatre. The curtain falls on Paul, and we see him next in prison. Of course, we have sensed the disaster coming. Like any playwright, Waugh prepares us for his best effects.

Further examples of the novelist's dramatic skill can be found in the prison scenes: Paul's walks with the 'lion of the Lord's elect' contrast his alarmed politeness to the grandiloquent fierceness of the visionary. Perhaps the best scene in the last part of the book is at the clinic where Alastair and the Fagan family celebrate Paul's 'death'. Waugh is always able to exploit theatrical opportunities in the story of *Decline and Fall*.

---

(3) Show how Waugh's use of language contributes to the comedy.

Decline and Fall is the work of a stylist. We soon recognise that every sentence is carefully planned. Enjoying the writing, we watch for the implications of words and phrases and pay close attention to what the characters say.

The narrative is elegant and polite, although the events related are frequently the opposite: that creates one kind of comedy. Waugh often uses understatement. On the first page he describes the 'roaring and breaking of glass' as the Bollinger Club proceeds with its dinner. Most of the academic staff are out of college: this evening, we are told, is a 'difficult time' for the authorities. Elsewhere the writing is epigrammatic. Some lines have become famous. The noise from the rooms of Sir Alastair Digby-Vane-Trumpington is dreadful: 'the sound of the English county families baying for broken glass' (on the second page). 'Baying' suggests the hounds used in fox-hunting—the county families' favourite pursuit. The normally respectable connotations of 'the English county families' clash amusingly with the vandalous connotations of the next phrase. Sometimes an epigram sums up both one character and the comic spirit of the whole novel. Dr Fagan's 'we schoolmasters must temper discretion with deceit' is funny because the responsible tone of a headmaster giving a young colleague advice fails to prepare us for the frankness of the last word. The principle expressed there pervades the novel: Fagan's words will often be remembered later on. Such neat, pointed use of language is a comic device.

The correct, polished prose of the story-telling is matched by the style in which some of the characters speak. Dr Fagan is always formal and dignified. Paul speaks fastidiously. Other people are given various dialects and species of slang, and Waugh finds humour in the discordancies produced. Paul's politeness is incongruous in prison: 'are you here for long?' he asks the prisoner he is set to walk with, as though at a hotel or a country house. 'This is a silly dodge,' the convict comments, and goes on in racy, idiomatic lines to tell Paul about prison life.

His normal speech patterns are followed by the exotic, biblical language of the carpenter who afterwards murders Prendergast. 'Lion of the Lord's elect', 'a sign to Israel', 'smiting the Philistine', 'Whore of Babylon', 'Moabite', 'washpot'—fragments of Bible-reading—appear in the deranged man's speech mixed with uneducated syntax and every-day idioms. To Paul this is frightening; to the reader it is entertaining; to the prison-warder it is 'language prejudicial to good discipline'. The warders' frequent misuse of prison terminology contrasts with the Governor's sociological diction. A properly used 'observation cell' is, the warders think, an instrument of torture.

Language often reflects the occasion. Prison is absurd to Paul and its various registers mingle absurdly. The grotesque death of Prendergast is reported in the chapel under cover of a hymn—'O God our help in ages past'. The familiar words and rhythms of the hymn are grotesquely punctuated by the convicts' news. The last and greatest absurdity of Paul's death is conveyed in the drunken speeches of the doctor who signs his death-certificate.

Waugh finds comedy in all forms of official language. At the schol-astic agency Llanabba is classified: 'Status of school: *school*.' That status is explained by Mr Levy. There are four classes of school: 'Leading School', 'First-rate School', 'Good School' and 'School'. 'School' is 'pretty bad'. Waugh is amused by the way that official terms can hide reality so discreetly. Public language is far more misleading at Grimes's wedding, where the vicar speaks movingly on 'Home and conjugal love'. 'How beautiful it is to see two young people in the hope of youth setting out with the Church's blessing to face life together . . .'. It is even more beautiful, he goes on, when in 'full manhood and woman-hood' two people say that life has taught them: '*one* is not enough'. Waugh relishes these ecclesiastical cadences for their own sake. They are comic here because so inappropriate to the circumstances. Potts's letters to Paul discuss educational theories in modish terms which are inappropriate to conditions at Llanabba. His second letter talks of 'new methods—to induce co-ordination of the senses'. Children have objects placed in their mouths; then make red chalk sketches of the shapes. Has Paul tried this? 'Are your colleagues enlightened?' Waugh is amused by how unenlightened Grimes and Prendergast are; and by Potts's inexperience. He had a sharp ear for incongruity in language. As a comic novelist he found situations in which to make our absurdities of usage ludicrously plain.

Minor topics

(1) Write on possessions in *Decline and Fall.*

Fortune is a theme of the novel; that anything can happen to anybody is a comic principle. Waugh's is a world of risk. The characters include the very rich Margot, and Prendergast who has almost nothing. All are in danger. The economic uncertainty of the time perhaps influenced Waugh, although he was not interested in economics. Certainly his own insecure life after leaving Oxford affected his view of possessions; he had rich friends and hoped to be rich himself; he was often in debt. He also believed that worldly goods—and all good fortune—are precarious.

The story begins with the stripping of Paul Pennyfeather of his clothes and his place at Oxford. Happily cycling back to college, he may have thought himself secure. The novelist asserts that nobody ever is. Having lived at Scone among the affluent, he finds himself among impoverished schoolmasters. Dingy tells him that masters are not provided with soap or bootpolish. Dr Fagan spends money on Sports Day, but when he thinks of buying Mr Prendergast a new tie, Dingy declares that such extravagance would be 'sinful'. Waugh does not seem angry about the disparity of wealth, although Fagan's income is thirty times that of Prendergast. He sees it as one absurdity among many others.

Paul's fortunes rise again for a time. At King's Thursday he meets people richer than he has ever known, although most of Margot's guests are reluctant to lose small sums at cards. Margot treats her possessions lightly: a house four hundred years old is demolished, rebuilt, and then demolished and rebuilt again, at whim. In the scene where she interviews girls for South America we see the shrewdness which brings such wealth, and the stark contrast between her corruptly financed life with Paul and the life of such women as Mrs Grimes. Margot reminds Paul that possessions mean work; but she would not be poor, she says, 'for all the ease in the world'. Unused to wealth on this scale, Paul makes a few minor purchases after their engagement; Margot is to allow him two thousand pounds a year. This section of the novel looks quizzically at great possessions.

In prison Paul is relieved of all he has. Some of his personal property is beyond the comprehension of the warder who takes charge of it: he has never seen a cigar-piercer (Paul's is gold, a gift from Alastair); the tie-pin—which he calls 'fancy'—was a gift from Margot and cost more than the warder earns in a year. Paul feels a pleasant irresponsibility after this second stripping. He settles easily into the possessionless life of prison. But even there, it soon turns out, Margot's influence can extend.

Caviare appears in the dish in his cell; brand new novels arrive from London; the doctor prescribes sherry. He is glad of the sherry, and glad later to be out of prison and in Margot's villa at Corfu. He accepts good fortune and bad. It is implied that his independence of possessions is an aspect of his temperament rather than a virtue. Margot is different.

At the close of the book Fortune has restored him to his old life of cocoa and books—as if acknowledging his relative indifference to her. But Paul has resolved now to keep away from the social 'wheel' on which possessions are pursued. That is a farcical, dangerous game. It does not suit him.

---

(2) Is religious belief treated seriously?

The adult Evelyn Waugh never scoffed at religious belief, although he disagreed sharply with non-Catholics. As a boy he was devout; as an adolescent he disbelieved. By 1925 he was considering becoming a clergyman. In 1930 he became a Roman Catholic. His Christian faith appears directly in most of his books written after 1945, but not in the prewar novels. In *Decline and Fall* his attitude to religion is not made clear.

Paul is a theology student at Scone, preparing to be a clergyman in the Church of England. His beliefs are unshaken by his adventures. Perhaps his patient, cheerful acceptance of solitary confinement in prison is made easier by his faith, but Waugh does not say so. Paul sympathises with Prendergast's situation after the arrival of 'doubts'; he makes no attempt to remove them. Nor does he condemn Grimes's vice, although we might have expected an ordinand to do so. We must remember that Paul, away from Scone and his normal life, is only 'a shadow'. He and the other characters are too flimsy for their religious experience to be treated seriously. The young Waugh did not consider piety a proper subject for his sort of fiction.

The college chaplain at Scone, and Prendergast's bishop who could not say why God created the world and didn't think the question need affect a rector's duties, are treated satirically. Even the later, more explicitly pious Waugh was prepared to make jokes about clergymen. Prendergast as a Modern Churchman, who acts as chaplain while still doubting, is treated scornfully, and is soon cut down by a genuine though insane believer. Waugh was always intolerant of what he saw as feeble-mindedness among Christians, and always intrigued by madness.

The 'lion of the Lord's elect' is very funny, and perhaps embarrassingly so to some devout readers. The joke is almost purely linguistic. Old Testament language, in the English translation of 1611, can be comical when taken out of context. When the aggrieved warder complains to the Governor that he has been called 'a Moabite' and 'a washpot', he doesn't know that the Old Testament declares Moab (an enemy territory and source of religious contamination) to be God's washpot—a worthless thing. These terms, full of meaning to the mad carpenter, are meaningless in a modern prison. Waugh perhaps implies agreement with the vicar's view at the Llanabba sports that excessive interest by lay people in religious matters endangers sanity.

There is little sign in *Decline and Fall* of Waugh's attitude to religious belief, serious or otherwise. We would assume, from the author's knowledge of biblical and ecclesiastical matters, that he took an interest in religion.

Part 5

Suggestions for further reading

The text

Decline and Fall: An Illustrated Novelette was first published by Chapman and Hall, London, 1928. This edition has line drawings by the author and has often been reprinted. A paperback version is published by Penguin Books, Harmondsworth, 1937, which is reprinted annually.

Other works by Evelyn Waugh

Waugh's novels are published in hardback by Chapman and Hall, London, and are also available in Penguin. The following novels are recommended for students of *Decline and Fall*:

Vile Bodies, 1930
A Handful of Dust, 1934
Scoop: A Novel About Journalists, 1938
The Loved One: An Anglo-American Tragedy, 1948
The 'Sword of Honour' trilogy:
  Men at Arms, 1952
  Officers and Gentlemen, 1955
  Unconditional Surrender, 1961

The first volume of Waugh's autobiography *A Little Learning*, Chapman and Hall, London, 1964, is useful background reading.

Criticism and relevant books

BOULTON, MARJORIE: *The Anatomy of the Novel*, Routledge and Kegan Paul, London and Boston, 1975. This is a good introduction to the study of fiction.

BRADBURY, MALCOLM: *Evelyn Waugh* (Writers and Critics series), Oliver and Boyd, Edinburgh and London, 1964

GREENBLATT, STEPHEN: *Three Modern Satirists: Waugh, Orwell and Huxley*, Yale University Press, London and New Haven, 1965

HOLLIS, CHRISTOPHER: *Evelyn Waugh*, Writers and their Work series, Longman for the British Council, Harlow, 1971

LODGE, DAVID: *Evelyn Waugh*, Essays on Modern Writers series, Columbia University Press, London and New York, 1971

PRYCE-JONES, DAVID (ED.): *Evelyn Waugh and his World*, Weidenfeld and Nicolson, London, 1973

SYKES, CHRISTOPHER: *Evelyn Waugh: A Biography*, Collins, London, 1975

The author of these notes

NEIL MCEWAN was educated at Pembroke College, Oxford. He has taught at universities in England, Canada and Africa, and is at present Lecturer in English at the University of Qatar. He has written the York Notes on D.H. Lawrence's *Women in Love*; Henry James's *Daisy Miller* and *The Europeans*; L.P. Hartley's *The Go-Between*; and the York Handbooks *Preparing for Examinations in English Literature* and *Style in English Prose*. He is the author of *The Survival of the Novel* (Macmillan) and *Africa and the Novel* (Macmillan).

York Notes: list of titles

CHINUA ACHEBE
A Man of the People
Arrow of God
Things Fall Apart

EDWARD ALBEE
Who's Afraid of Virginia Woolf?

ELECHI AMADI
The Concubine

ANONYMOUS
Beowulf
Everyman

AYI KWEI ARMAH
The Beautyful Ones Are Not Yet Born

W. H. AUDEN
Selected Poems

JANE AUSTEN
Emma
Mansfield Park
Northanger Abbey
Persuasion
Pride and Prejudice
Sense and Sensibility

HONORÉ DE BALZAC
Le Père Goriot

SAMUEL BECKETT
Waiting for Godot

SAUL BELLOW
Henderson, The Rain King

ARNOLD BENNETT
Anna of the Five Towns
The Card

WILLIAM BLAKE
Songs of Innocence, Songs of Experience

ROBERT BOLT
A Man For All Seasons

HAROLD BRIGHOUSE
Hobson's Choice

ANNE BRONTË
The Tenant of Wildfell Hall

CHARLOTTE BRONTË
Jane Eyre

EMILY BRONTË
Wuthering Heights

ROBERT BROWNING
Men and Women

JOHN BUCHAN
The Thirty-Nine Steps

JOHN BUNYAN
The Pilgrim's Progress

BYRON
Selected Poems

ALBERT CAMUS
L'Etranger (The Outsider)

GEOFFREY CHAUCER
Prologue to the Canterbury Tales
The Clerk's Tale
The Franklin's Tale
The Knight's Tale
The Merchant's Tale
The Miller's Tale
The Nun's Priest's Tale
The Pardoner's Tale
The Wife of Bath's Tale
Troilus and Criseyde

ANTON CHEKOV
The Cherry Orchard

SAMUEL TAYLOR COLERIDGE
Selected Poems

WILKIE COLLINS
The Moonstone

SIR ARTHUR CONAN DOYLE
The Hound of the Baskervilles

WILLIAM CONGREVE
The Way of the World

JOSEPH CONRAD
Heart of Darkness
Lord Jim
Nostromo
The Secret Agent
Victory
Youth and *Typhoon*

STEPHEN CRANE
The Red Badge of Courage

BRUCE DAWE
Selected Poems

WALTER DE LA MARE
Selected Poems

DANIEL DEFOE
A Journal of the Plague Year
Moll Flanders
Robinson Crusoe

CHARLES DICKENS
A Tale of Two Cities
Bleak House
David Copperfield
Dombey and Son
Great Expectations
Hard Times
Little Dorrit
Oliver Twist
Our Mutual Friend
The Pickwick Papers

EMILY DICKINSON
Selected Poems

JOHN DONNE
Selected Poems

JOHN DRYDEN
Selected Poems

GERALD DURRELL
My Family and Other Animals

GEORGE ELIOT
Adam Bede
Middlemarch
Silas Marner
The Mill on the Floss

T. S. ELIOT
Four Quartets
Murder in the Cathedral
Selected Poems
The Cocktail Party
The Waste Land

J. G. FARRELL
The Siege of Krishnapur

GEORGE FARQUHAR
The Beaux Stratagem

WILLIAM FAULKNER
Absalom, Absalom!
The Sound and the Fury

HENRY FIELDING
Joseph Andrews
Tom Jones

F. SCOTT FITZGERALD
Tender is the Night
The Great Gatsby

GUSTAVE FLAUBERT
Madame Bovary

E. M. FORSTER
A Passage to India
Howards End

JOHN FOWLES
The French Lieutenant's Woman

ATHOL FUGARD
Selected Plays

JOHN GALSWORTHY
Strife

MRS GASKELL
North and South

WILLIAM GOLDING
Lord of the Flies
The Spire

OLIVER GOLDSMITH
She Stoops to Conquer
The Vicar of Wakefield

ROBERT GRAVES
Goodbye to All That

GRAHAM GREENE
Brighton Rock
The Heart of the Matter
The Power and the Glory

WILLIS HALL
The Long and the Short and the Tall

THOMAS HARDY
Far from the Madding Crowd
Jude the Obscure
Selected Poems
Tess of the D'Urbervilles
The Mayor of Casterbridge
The Return of the Native
The Trumpet Major
The Woodlanders
Under the Greenwood Tree

L. P. HARTLEY
The Go-Between
The Shrimp and the Anemone

NATHANIEL HAWTHORNE
The Scarlet Letter

SEAMUS HEANEY
Selected Poems

JOSEPH HELLER
Catch-22

ERNEST HEMINGWAY
A Farewell to Arms
For Whom the Bell Tolls
The Old Man and the Sea

GEORGE HERBERT
Selected Poems

HERMANN HESSE
Steppenwolf

BARRY HINES
Kes

HOMER
The Iliad
The Odyssey

ANTHONY HOPE
The Prisoner of Zenda

GERARD MANLEY HOPKINS
Selected Poems

WILLIAM DEAN HOWELLS
The Rise of Silas Lapham

RICHARD HUGHES
A High Wind in Jamaica

TED HUGHES
Selected Poems

THOMAS HUGHES
Tom Brown's Schooldays

ALDOUS HUXLEY
Brave New World

HENRIK IBSEN
A Doll's House
Ghosts

HENRY JAMES
Daisy Miller
The Ambassadors
The Europeans
The Portrait of a Lady
The Turn of the Screw
Washington Square

SAMUEL JOHNSON
Rasselas

BEN JONSON
The Alchemist
Volpone

JAMES JOYCE
A Portrait of the Artist as a Young Man
Dubliners

JOHN KEATS
Selected Poems

RUDYARD KIPLING
Kim

D. H. LAWRENCE
Sons and Lovers
The Rainbow
Women in Love

CAMARA LAYE
L'Enfant Noir

HARPER LEE
To Kill a Mocking-Bird

LAURIE LEE
Cider with Rosie

THOMAS MANN
Tonio Kröger

CHRISTOPHER MARLOWE
Doctor Faustus

ANDREW MARVELL
Selected Poems

W. SOMERSET MAUGHAM
Selected Short Stories

GAVIN MAXWELL
Ring of Bright Water

J. MEADE FALKNER
Moonfleet

HERMAN MELVILLE
Billy Budd
Moby Dick

THOMAS MIDDLETON
Women Beware Women

THOMAS MIDDLETON and WILLIAM ROWLEY
The Changeling

ARTHUR MILLER
A View from the Bridge
Death of a Salesman
The Crucible

JOHN MILTON
Paradise Lost I & II
Paradise Lost IV & IX
Selected Poems

V. S. NAIPAUL
A House for Mr Biswas

ROBERT O'BRIEN
Z for Zachariah

SEAN O'CASEY
Juno and the Paycock

GABRIEL OKARA
The Voice

EUGENE O'NEILL
Mourning Becomes Electra

GEORGE ORWELL
Animal Farm
Nineteen Eighty-four

JOHN OSBORNE
Look Back in Anger

WILFRED OWEN
Selected Poems

ALAN PATON
Cry, The Beloved Country

THOMAS LOVE PEACOCK
Nightmare Abbey and *Crotchet Castle*

HAROLD PINTER
The Caretaker

PLATO
The Republic

ALEXANDER POPE
Selected Poems

J. B. PRIESTLEY
An Inspector Calls

THOMAS PYNCHON
The Crying of Lot 49

SIR WALTER SCOTT
Ivanhoe
Quentin Durward
The Heart of Midlothian
Waverley

PETER SHAFFER
The Royal Hunt of the Sun

WILLIAM SHAKESPEARE
A Midsummer Night's Dream
Antony and Cleopatra
As You Like It
Coriolanus
Cymbeline
Hamlet
Henry IV Part I
Henry IV Part II
Henry V
Julius Caesar
King Lear
Love's Labour's Lost
Macbeth
Measure for Measure
Much Ado About Nothing
Othello
Richard II
Richard III
Romeo and Juliet
Sonnets
The Merchant of Venice
The Taming of the Shrew
The Tempest
The Winter's Tale
Troilus and Cressida
Twelfth Night

GEORGE BERNARD SHAW
Androcles and the Lion
Arms and the Man
Caesar and Cleopatra
Candida
Major Barbara
Pygmalion
Saint Joan
The Devil's Disciple

MARY SHELLEY
Frankenstein

PERCY BYSSHE SHELLEY
Selected Poems

RICHARD BRINSLEY SHERIDAN
The School for Scandal
The Rivals

R. C. SHERRIFF
Journey's End

WOLE SOYINKA
The Road
Three Short Plays

EDMUND SPENSER
The Faerie Queene (Book I)

JOHN STEINBECK
Of Mice and Men
The Grapes of Wrath
The Pearl

LAURENCE STERNE
A Sentimental Journey
Tristram Shandy

ROBERT LOUIS STEVENSON
Kidnapped
Treasure Island
Dr Jekyll and Mr Hyde

TOM STOPPARD
Professional Foul
Rosencrantz and Guildenstern are Dead

JONATHAN SWIFT
Gulliver's Travels

JOHN MILLINGTON SYNGE
The Playboy of the Western World

TENNYSON
Selected Poems

W. M. THACKERAY
Vanity Fair

DYLAN THOMAS
Under Milk Wood

EDWARD THOMAS
Selected Poems

FLORA THOMPSON
Lark Rise to Candleford

J. R. R. TOLKIEN
The Hobbit
The Lord of the Rings

ANTHONY TROLLOPE
Barchester Towers

MARK TWAIN
Huckleberry Finn
Tom Sawyer

JOHN VANBRUGH
The Relapse

VIRGIL
The Aeneid

VOLTAIRE
Candide

KEITH WATERHOUSE
Billy Liar

EVELYN WAUGH
Decline and Fall

JOHN WEBSTER
The Duchess of Malfi
The White Devil

H. G. WELLS
The History of Mr Polly
The Invisible Man
The War of the Worlds

OSCAR WILDE
The Importance of Being Earnest

THORNTON WILDER
Our Town

TENNESSEE WILLIAMS
The Glass Menagerie

VIRGINIA WOOLF
Mrs Dalloway
To the Lighthouse

WILLIAM WORDSWORTH
Selected Poems

WILLIAM WYCHERLEY
The Country Wife

W. B. YEATS
Selected Poems